Collaborative Library Lessons for the
Primary Grades

Collaborative Library Lessons for the Primary Grades

Linking Research Skills to Curriculum Standards

Written and Illustrated by
Brenda S. Copeland and Patricia A. Messner

LIBRARIES
UNLIMITED
A Member of the Greenwood Publishing Group

Westport, Connecticut • London

British Library Cataloguing in Publication Data is available.

ISBN: 1–59158–185–0

First published in 2004

Libraries Unlimited, 88 Post Road West, Westport, CT 06881
A Member of the Greenwood Publishing Group, Inc.
www.lu.com

Printed in the United States of America

The paper used in this book complies with the Permanent Paper Standard issued by the National Information Standards Organization (Z39.48-1984).

10 9 8 7 6 5 4 3 2 1

The authors and publisher gratefully acknowledge permission to use the following materials:

Standards for the English Language Arts, by the International Reading Association and the National Council of Teachers of English, Copyright 1996 by the International Reading Association and the National Council of Teachers of English. Reprinted with permission.

National Standards for History Grades K-4 from the National Center for History in the Schools reprinted with permission.

Reprinted with permission from National Science Education Standards © 1996 by the National Academy of Sciences, courtesy of the National Academies Press, Washington, DC.

Dedicated to our children, Carol, Jim, Bill, Dan, Sara, and Mark, the real technology gurus in our lives.

Contents

Part Four:
Atlas Unit

Part Five:
Online Catalog Unit

Part Six:
Internet Unit

Part Seven:
Thematic Unit

Introduction

Over our years as elementary media specialists, we have concentrated on crafting lesson plans that enable our older elementary students to do research efficiently and effectively and use current technologies. Ironically, it is the younger students who pour over the pages of books in our reference section. They beg to look up information on the computer and ask to take home the big reference books with all the cool animal pictures. Many enthusiastic exchanges can be overheard from this quiet corner of the library.

In this book of lesson plans and worksheets, we have taken the traditional lessons usually reserved for fourth, fifth, and sixth graders and redesigned them for second and third. Our goal was to keep them simple and introduce the subjects so that excitement for learning awesome facts would be fanned into a healthy hunger for knowledge and understanding.

We also feel strongly that library instruction needs to expand to include the classroom teacher in as many collaborative curricular activities as possible. Research is telling us that this collaborative team approach pays big dividends in terms of higher test scores, but, more important, in the shaping of a child's entire educational experience. Our children will have to compete in a high-tech global world and as educators (classroom teachers and media specialists) we need to do everything we can to prepare them to meet the challenge.

Each lesson has ready-to-use worksheets and is aligned with national standards. The Language Arts Standards are from the National Council of Teachers of English. They can be found at www.ncte.org and also in Standards for the English Language Arts sponsored by the National Council of Teacher of English and International Reading Association (Urbana, IL: NCTE, 1996). The Science Standards were taken from *National Science Education Standards* (Washington DC: National Academy Press, 1996). The Social Studies Standards are from the National Council for the Social Studies. They can be found at www.sscnet.ucla.edu/nchs/ and www.nationalgeographic.com. The Geography Standards are from *Geography for Life* (Collingdale, Pa: Diane Publishing Company, 1994).

There are seven units in the book: thematic, biography, atlas, almanac, encyclopedia, online catalog, and the Internet. The lessons are written for a forty-five-minute class time and they coordinate both classroom and media time. Each lesson lists the applicable national standard and provides objectives, skills, materials, and pages for overhead transparencies.

When using overhead transparencies out of printed materials, remember the fair-use issue. Educators may use overheads for a year, but after the year is up will need to make new ones using new materials. Even though these lessons can be adapted to be taught completely by the media specialist, we challenge you to work on them as a team and watch the seeds of collaboration blossom.

The Standards

Standards for the English Language Arts

NL-ENG.K-12.2 UNDERSTANDING THE HUMAN EXPERIENCE

Students read a wide range of literature from many periods in many genres to build an understanding of many dimensions of human experience.

NL-ENG.K-12.3 EVALUATION STRATEGIES

Students apply a wide range of strategies to comprehend, interpret, evaluate, and appreciate texts. They draw on their prior experience, their interactions with other readers and writers, their knowledge of word meaning and of other texts, their word identification strategies, and their understanding of textual features (e.g., sound-letter correspondence, sentence structure, context, graphics).

NL-ENG.K-12.4 COMMUNICATION SKILLS

Students adjust their use of spoken, written, and visual language (e.g., conventions, style, vocabulary) to communicate effectively with a variety of audiences and for different purposes.

NL-ENG.K-12.5 COMMUNICATION STRATEGIES

Students employ a wide range of strategies as they write and use different writing process elements appropriately to communicate with different audiences for a variety of purposes.

NL-ENG.K12.6 APPLYING KNOWLEDGE

Students apply knowledge of language structure, language conventions (e.g., spelling and punctuation), media techniques, figurative language, and genre to create, critique, and discuss print and nonprint texts.

NL-ENG.K-12.8 DEVELOPING RESEARCH SKILLS

Students use a variety of technological and information resources (e.g., libraries, databases, computer networks, video) to gather and synthesize information and to create and communicate knowledge.

NL-ENG.K-12.12 APPLYING LANGUAGE SKILLS

Students use spoken, written, and visual language to accomplish their own purpose (e.g., for learning, enjoyment, persuasion, and the exchange of information).

National Standards for Geography

NSS-G.K-12.1 THE WORLD IN SPATIAL TERMS

As a result of activities in grades K–12, all students should: Understand how to use maps and other geographic representations, tools, and technologies to acquire, process, and report information from a spatial perspective.

National Standards for History

NSS-USH.K-4.1 LIVING AND WORKING TOGETHER IN FAMILIES AND COMMUNITIES, NOW AND LONG AGO

Understands family life now and in the past, and family life in various places long ago. Understands the history of the local community and how communities in North America varied long ago.

Science National Standards

NS.K-4.3 LIFE SCIENCE

As a result of activities in Grades K–4, all students should develop understanding of

- The characteristics of organisms
- Life cycles of organisms
- Organisms and environments

Part One

Biography
Unit

Lesson 1—Library/Media Center

Tea with Eleanor Roosevelt

Objective: Students will be able to learn the definition and location of both individual and collective biographies. They will also be able to recognize facts about Eleanor Roosevelt.

Language Arts National Standards

NL-ENG.K-12.2 UNDERSTANDING THE HUMAN EXPERIENCE

Students read a wide range of literature from many periods in many genres to build an understanding of the many dimensions (e.g., philosophical, ethical, aesthetic) of human experience.

NL-ENG. K-12.3 EVALUATION STRATEGIES

Students apply a wide range of strategies to comprehend, interpret, evaluate, and appreciate texts. They draw on their prior experience, their interactions with other readers and writers, their knowledge of word meaning and of other texts, their word identification strategies, and their understanding of textual features (e.g., sound-letter correspondence, sentence structure, context graphics).

Skills

- Word identification and definition
- Biography study, both individual and collective

Costume

- Paisley belted dress
- Ladies 1930s dress hat
- Black lace-up heeled shoes

    (Check your local thrift store for these items)

Props

- Teapot, teacups, tray, and fancy napkins

Materials

- Tea bags (see instruction sheet for sample)
- Word cards labeled "collective biography," "individual biography," and "call numbers" (see sheet of words and definitions)
- Collections of books about Eleanor Roosevelt, both individual and collective biography.

3

Step 1. The media specialist greets the students dressed as Eleanor Roosevelt. Welcome them to your tea party. Explain to the students that you are dressed as Eleanor Roosevelt and you are going to introduce them to the world of biographies. Share the facts about Eleanor using the tea bags (see tea bag example) and to aid your storytelling as you point out the highlights of her life. Be dramatic with your presentation. Your students will enjoy your playacting, and it will get them hooked on the biography section. The tea fact cards are only a sample of the many facts about this famous first lady.

Step 2. After the presentation, introduce the word cards for individual and collective biographies. Explain that we can read about Mrs. Roosevelt in both types of books. Share the books that you have gathered ahead of time.

Step 3. Explain the call numbers.

> **Individual** 92—Dewey number
>
> > Roo—Person you wish to read about
>
> **Collective** 920—Dewey number
>
> > Adl—Author's last name

Closure. Walk students through the biography section and point out where the Eleanor Roosevelt books are located. Pick out a few famous people that students will recognize and point these out also. Spend time helping them select a book to take back to the classroom.

Teacher's Notes:

Biography Unit
Lesson 1

Sample Tea Bag

Directions:

Cut the fact cards apart (see fact card page) and mount on heavier paper.

Cut smaller squares from colored construction paper and attach the numbered square to the fact squares using string. Place the tea bags inside the teapot, allowing the numbered squares to hang out like a regular tea bag. As you tell the story of Eleanor, pull the tea bags from the pot and use the facts to help you remember the important highlights of her life that you wish to stress.

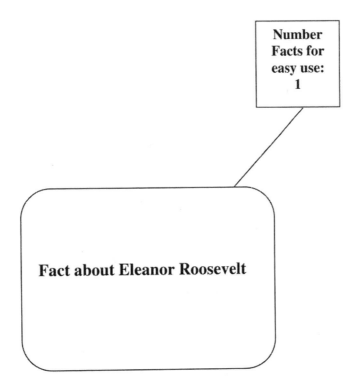

Number Facts for easy use: 1

Fact about Eleanor Roosevelt

Sample Tea Bag Facts

1. Eleanor was not considered beautiful, and she lacked self-confidence. She was the niece of the twenty-sixth president, Theodore Roosevelt.	2. She fell in love with Franklin Roosevelt. He was a distant cousin, so when they were married, she did not have to change her name.	3. Eleanor and Franklin had six children. One son died when just a baby.
4. Her husband ran for governor of New York. Eleanor helped him win. They worked as a team. Many times Eleanor went out to talk with the people on Franklin's behalf.	5. Franklin came down with polio and Eleanor helped nurse him back to health. With Eleanor's help, he was able to solve many problems as governor of New York.	6. Some people wanted to see Franklin become president of the United States. He was elected in 1932, and Eleanor became the first lady of the United States.
7. When our country went to war after Pearl Harbor, Eleanor visited factories and even traveled to see the soldiers.	8. Franklin Roosevelt died before peace came. Eleanor still worked for her country by helping the poor.	9. She died November 7, 1962. She loved to help others, and by doing so, she brought much happiness to her own life.

Word and Definition Cards

Cut, enlarge, and paste onto construction paper.

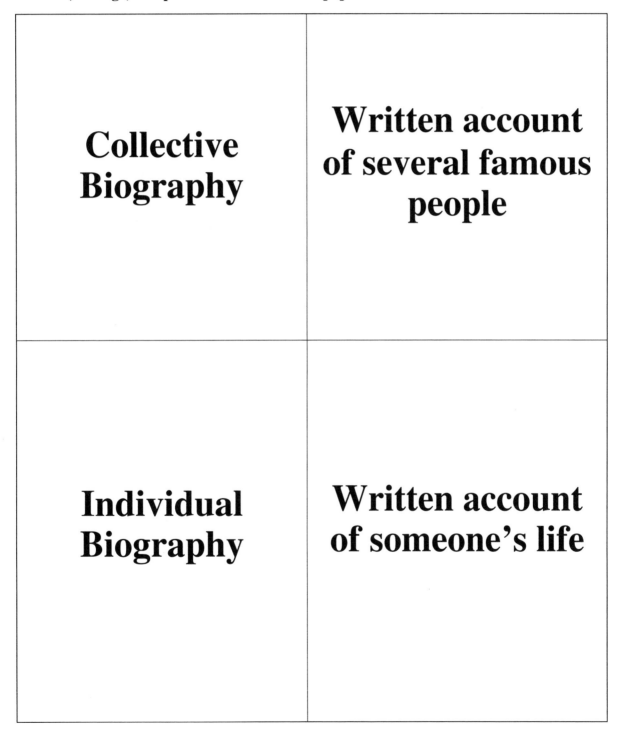

| Collective Biography | Written account of several famous people |
| Individual Biography | Written account of someone's life |

Name_____ Age_____

Where do you live?_____

_____

Do you have any brothers? If yes, what are their names?_____

_____

Do you have any sisters? If yes, what are their names?_____

_____

What stuffed animal or toy do you have that is special?_____

What is your favorite subject at school?_____

What are you going to be when you grow up?_____

_____

Do you have a pet? If so, what kind?_____

_____

What is your pet's name?_____

_____

What is something you don't like?_____

_____

What is your favorite color?_____

What sport do you like to play?_____

_____

Person who did this interview_____

_____

Third Grade Interview Sheet

Name_____Age_____

What is your favorite color?_____

Do you have any brothers? If yes, what are their names?_____

_____

Do you have any sisters? If yes, what are their names?_____

_____

What is your address?_____

_____

What is your favorite book character?_____

_____

What is your favorite subject in school?_____

_____

What do you like to do with your best friend?_____

_____

What kind of books do you enjoy reading?_____

_____

What is something special about you?_____

_____

What is something you are good at?_____

_____

Person who did this interview_____

_____

**Call Numbers Worksheet
Second Grade**

Directions: Underline the title of the book. Finish the call number in the box.

Example:

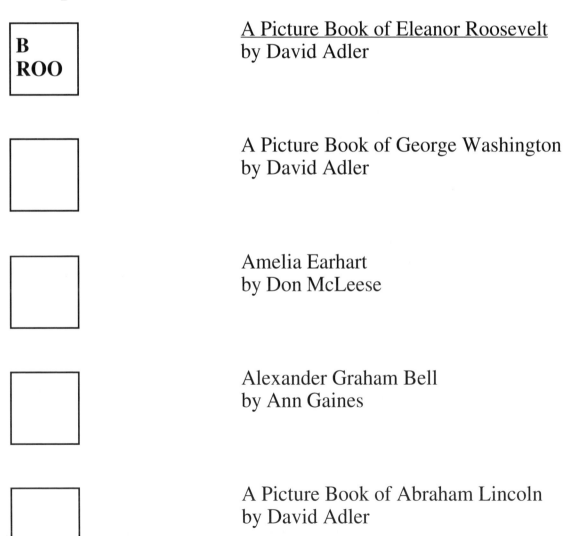

B **ROO**	<u>A Picture Book of Eleanor Roosevelt</u> by David Adler
	A Picture Book of George Washington by David Adler
	Amelia Earhart by Don McLeese
	Alexander Graham Bell by Ann Gaines
	A Picture Book of Abraham Lincoln by David Adler

Third Grade Worksheet

Call Numbers Worksheet
Third Grade

Directions: Underline the title and circle the last name of who the book is about. Finish the call number in the box.

Example:

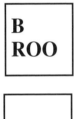

A Picture Book of Eleanor Roosevelt
by David Adler

A Picture Book of George Washington
by David Adler

Amelia Earhart
by Don McLeese

Alexander Graham Bell
by Ann Gaines

A Picture Book of Abraham Lincoln
by David Adler

Bonus Question

First Ladies: Women Who Called the White House Home
by Beatrice Gormley

Lesson 3—Classroom
Timeline

Objective: Second-grade students will gather information about a person and place the information on a timeline. Third-grade students will gather information about a person and sort into four categories: early years, marriage and family, important events, and later years.

Social Studies National Standards

NSS-USH.K-4.1 LIVING AND WORKING TOGETHER IN FAMILIES AND COMMUNITIES, NOW AND LONG AGO

Understands family life now and in the past, and family life in various places long ago. Understands the history of the local community and how communities in North America varied long ago.

Skills
- Note taking
- Organization of information

Materials
- An easy biography to read aloud
- Dry eraser board and markers
- Timeline
- Chart of four categories (see pattern)

Step 1. Read the book *A Picture Book of Amelia Earhart* by David Adler to the class. Before reading the biography, review the definition of a biography from Lesson 1. Also tell the students that they will need to listen for important facts during the read-aloud.

Step 2. Students will recall facts from the read-aloud and write the facts on the dry erase board.

Step 3. Second Grade: Introduce the purpose of a timeline. Model an example by placing dates and facts on the timeline. The example could be the teacher's life. Students will write facts from the read-aloud on paper and place them on the timeline.

Timeline Example

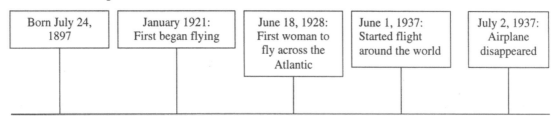

| Born July 24, 1897 | January 1921: First began flying | June 18, 1928: First woman to fly across the Atlantic | June 1, 1937: Started flight around the world | July 2, 1937: Airplane disappeared |

Step 4. Third Grade: Introduce the idea of sorting facts into four categories. Students write the facts from the board onto index cards. Enlarge the pattern and place on the dry erase board. Students will take turns placing the facts in the right category.

Closure. Review timeline and sorting of information. Introduce next lesson. Students will be going to the library/media center with a partner to gather facts about a person.

Biography Unit
Lesson 3

Sorting Pattern

Early Years   **Marriage and Family**

Important Events   **Later Years**

Lesson 4—Library/Media Center, Team Teaching

Sorting Information

Objective: Students will gather and sort information about a famous person.

Social Studies National Standards

NSS-USH.K-4.1 LIVING AND WORKING TOGETHER IN FAMILIES AND COMMUNITIES, NOW AND LONG AGO

Understands family life now and in the past, and family life in various places long ago. Understands the history of the local community and how communities in North America varied long ago.

Skills

- Note taking
- Organization of information

Materials

- An assortment of easy biography books (see resources at the end of unit)
- Third grade worksheet from Lesson 3 for every group of students
- Second grade timeline worksheet for every group of students

Step 1. The classroom teacher divides students into groups. The media specialist introduces the activity to the students. Explain that the students will read a short biography, and gather and sort facts.

Step 2. Each group of students selects a biography to read. While reading, students gather facts and complete the worksheet.

Step 3. The media specialist and classroom teacher rotate around the library/media center helping groups of students as needed.

Step 4. Students share their facts with the class.

Optional Activity: Students may complete their own timeline and share with the class. Students can use photographs or drawings to complete the timeline.

Biography Unit
Lesson 4

Second Grade Worksheet

Names: _____

Title: _____

Author: _____

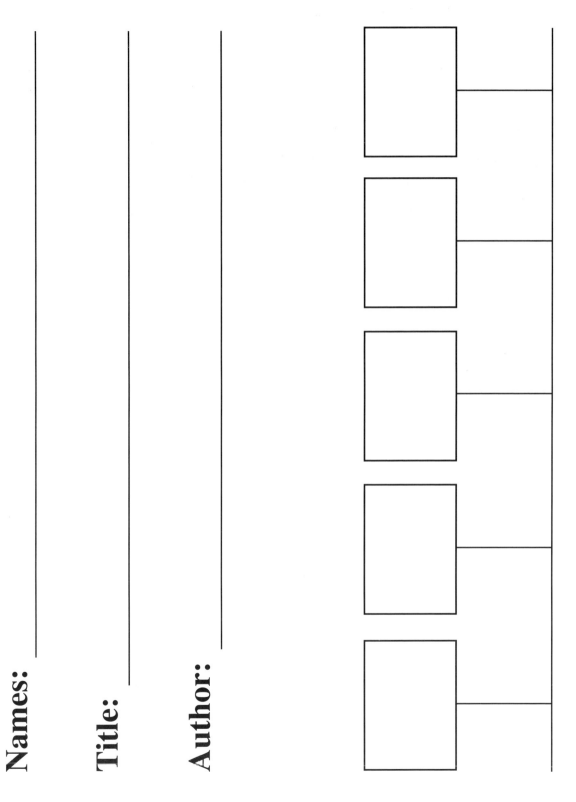

Lesson 5—Library/Media Center, Team Teaching

Selecting a Person for Research

Objective: Students will investigate the amount of information about several well-known people in the library/media center and select a person to research and complete a final project.

Social Studies National Standards

NSS-USH.K-4.1 LIVING AND WORKING TOGETHER IN FAMILIES AND COMMUNITIES, NOW AND LONG AGO

Understands family life now and in the past, and family life in various places long ago. Understands the history of the local community and how communities in North America varied long ago.

Skills

- Note taking
- Research—books and Internet

Step 1. The classroom teacher explains the final project assignment. The students select a well-known person to research and complete their projects. The final project can be an oral report with a costume or a written report with a poster or other visual aid.

Step 2. Students write down two people as possible subjects to research for their final projects.

Step 3. Students go to the library/media center.

Step 4. The classroom teacher explains the worksheet. Students gather sources for their reports. The media specialist explains the procedure for the time spent in the library/media center. Students are divided into three groups. Each group rotates around the library/media center investigating possible subjects for their projects. One group starts in the biography section, looking for biographies about its subjects. The next group starts in the encyclopedia section, looking for articles about its subjects. The last group starts on the computers, looking for pictures and articles of the people they may use for the final project. Students will use the worksheet to collect information.

Step 5. The classroom teacher and media specialist move around the library/media center helping students as needed.

Step 6. Students take their worksheets back to class and decide which person they are going to focus on for their final projects.

Biography Unit
Lesson 5

Final Project Worksheet

List of Possible People for Final Project

1._____

Biography Section

Title_____Author_____

Title_____Author_____

Encyclopedias

Volume_____Page_____

Volume_____Page_____

Computers

Web Sites_____

Web Sites_____

2._____

Biography Section

Title_____Author_____

Title_____Author_____

Encyclopedias

Volume_____Page_____

Volume_____Page_____

Computers

Web Sites_____

Web Sites_____

Lesson 6—Library/Media Center, Team Teaching

Research

Objective: Students will research a person for their final project.

Social Studies National Standards

NSS-USH.K-4.1 LIVING AND WORKING TOGETHER IN FAMILIES AND COMMUNITIES, NOW AND LONG AGO

Understands family life now and in the past, and family life in various places long ago. Understands the history of the local community and how communities in North America varied long ago.

Skills

- Note taking
- Research
- Sorting information

Materials

- Copies of sorting chart for each student

Step 1. The classroom teacher brings the students to the library/media center and explains the worksheet. Students gather facts, sort, and record sources. The media specialist explains the three areas in which the students will be working.

Step 2. Students find books, encyclopedias, and Web sites to gather information for their biography projects.

Step 3. In Lesson 5, students spent time using search engines. Students bring their worksheets from Lesson 5 and have decided which person to research. Students print articles and pictures from the Internet.

Step 4. Students begin to take notes and sort information, using the sorting worksheet. They also record their sources on the worksheet. Second graders record the author and title. Third graders record the author, title, publisher, and copyright date. All grades will record complete Web site addresses.

Step 5. Students may checkout books if a large collection of biography books are available.

Step 6. More time maybe needed if students do not checkout books. Books should be reserved for future visits to the library/media center.

Step 7. Students take information with them to complete project in the classroom and home.

Step 8. Students share their projects.

Early Years	**Marriage and Family**
Important Events	**Later Years**

Sources

Author_____ Title _____

Publisher _____ Copyright Date _____

Author _____Title _____

Publisher _____Copyright Date _____

Web Site _____

Web Site _____

Part Two

1	2	3	4	5	6	7	8	9	10	11	12	13	14	15	16	17	18	19	20	I N D E X
A	B	C	D	E	F	G	H	I	JK	L	M	N	O	P	QR	S	T	UV	WX YZ	

Encyclopedia Unit

Lesson 1—Library/Media Center

Introduction

Objective: Students will select the correct volume in a set of encyclopedias when given an assignment to find people, places, or things.

Language Arts National Standards

NL-ENG.K-12.3 EVALUATION STRATEGIES

Students apply a wide range of strategies to comprehend, interpret, evaluate, and appreciate texts. They draw on their prior experience, their interactions with other readers, and writers, their knowledge of word meaning and of other texts, their word identification strategies, and their understanding of textual features (e.g., sound-letter correspondence, sentence structure, context, graphics).

Skills

- Use of encyclopedia

Materials

- Word and definition cards for encyclopedia and call number (see word card page; enlarge and laminate)

- Overhead transparency about what is found in an encyclopedia

- Copies of second and third grade worksheets for each student

Step 1. As students enter the library/media center, the media specialist seats them in the reference section near the encyclopedias. Use the word and definition cards to introduce this group of reference works. Point out special encyclopedia sets also as well as general encyclopedias (e.g., Rourke's *World of Science Encyclopedia* and *The World Book Student Discovery Encyclopedia* are both great for second and third graders).

Step 2. Using the overhead transparency, discuss what can be found in a general encyclopedia. Brainstorm things that the students think might be found in a general encyclopedia. List their responses on the bottom of an overhead transparency.

Step 3. Explain the alphabetical arrangement of the sets. All of the "A" words would be in the first volume, and all of the "S" words would be in the S volume.

Step 4. Discuss proper names and how to look up names of a given person. Write several names on the board and practice looking up the names. The media specialist can hold the volume and show students how to look up the names.

Step 5. Go over the directions for the worksheet. Give students time to complete their worksheets.

Closure. Check answers as a group. As students prepare to leave, ask them which encyclopedia volume they would use to locate "snakes," "dogs," and "horses." Choose simple subjects for this. They can be written out on cards ahead of time if your class needs to see the words visually.

Word and Definition Cards

Cut, enlarge, and paste onto construction paper.

Encyclopedia	**A set of reference books that has general information on various subjects**
Call Number	**REF 030**

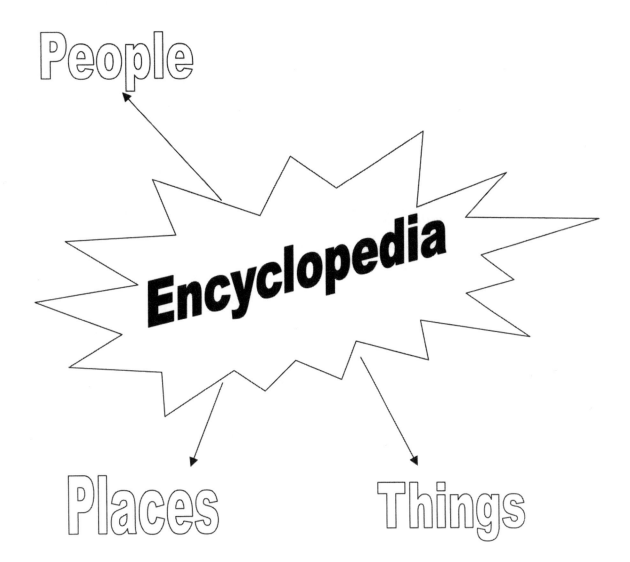

Examples:

People	Places	Things
1.	1.	1.
2.	2.	2.

Second Grade Worksheet

1	2	3	4	5	6	7	8	9	10	11	12	13	14	15	16	17	18	19	20	I N D E X
A	B	C	D	E	F	G	H	I	JK	L	M	N	O	P	QR	S	T	UV	WX YZ	X

Here is a set of encyclopedias. After each article title, list the volume where it would be found.

Rivers_____   Cheese_____

Volcanoes_____   Cats_____

Tigers_____   Dogs_____

Snakes_____   Fire_____

Planets_____   Violin_____

Bonus Question: In which volume would you find an article about George Washington? _____

Third Grade Worksheet

1	2	3	4	5	6	7	8	9	10	11	12	13	14	15	16	17	18	19	20	I N D E X
A	B	C	D	E	F	G	H	I	JK	L	M	N	O	P	QR	S	T	UV	WX YZ	X

Here is a set of encyclopedias. After each article title, list the volume where it would be found.

Rivers_____   Cheese_____

Volcanoes_____   Cats_____

Tigers_____   Dogs_____

South America_____   Ohio_____

Abe Lincoln_____   Alabama_____

George Bush_____   Electricity_____

Robert E. Lee_____   Disease_____

Lesson 2—Library/Media Center

Guide Words

Objective: Students use guide words to locate articles in the encyclopedia.

Language Arts National Standards

NL-ENG.K-12.3 EVALUATION STRATEGIES

Students apply a wide range of strategies to comprehend, interpret, evaluate, and appreciate texts. They draw on their prior experience, their interactions with other readers and writers, their knowledge of word meaning and of other texts, their word identification strategies, and their understanding of textual features (e.g., sound-letter correspondence, sentence structure, context, graphics).

Skills

- Using guide words in an encyclopedia

Materials

- Word and definition cards for encyclopedia and call number from Lesson 1
- Word and definition cards for guide words and volume (enlarge and laminate); see word card patterns
- Encyclopedias
- Copy a page from an encyclopedia and make it into an overhead transparency (use a page that has several small articles on one page)
- Guide page worksheet for each student

Step 1. Using the word cards from Lesson 1, review the basic points of the lesson previously covered.

Step 2. Explain the concept of using guide words to help locate articles or information faster. Use the word and definition cards at this time to help cement this concept. Share the overhead transparency of the page from the encyclopedia and model finding one of the articles on the page. Stress the fact that all of the words in this volume start with the same letter and that students will need to go to the second or third letter in alphabetical order to help in the location process.

Step 3. Allow time for practice with the encyclopedias. Pair up students and have them look up articles from the encyclopedias that you have selected and written on the board.

Step 4. Guided practice: Go over the directions for the worksheets and allow time for completion of work.

Closure. Exchange papers and have students correct them so they can see their mistakes. Reinforce the correct answers in any places that students found difficult.

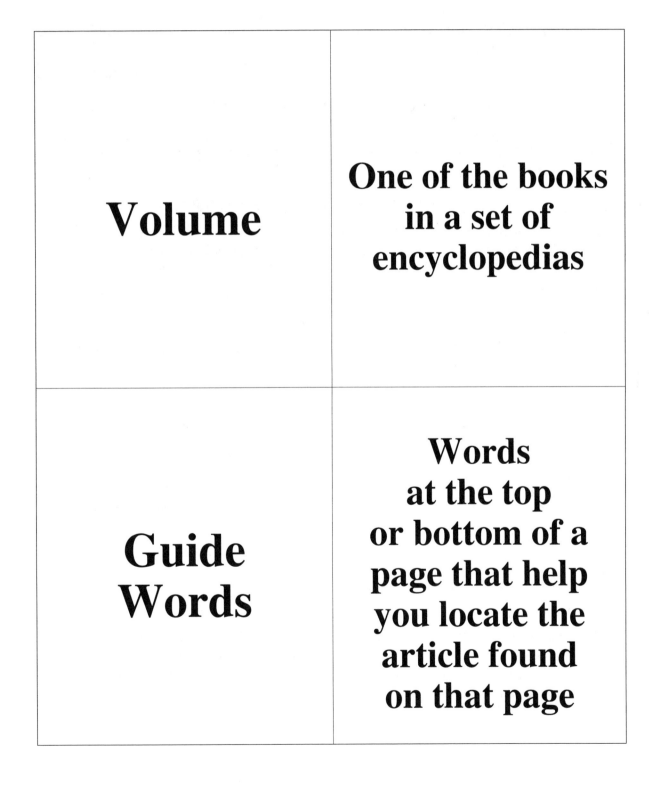

Volume	**One of the books in a set of encyclopedias**
Guide Words	**Words at the top or bottom of a page that help you locate the article found on that page**

Second Grade Guide Word Worksheet

Use the guide words at the top of the page to help you decide which words would belong on these encyclopedia pages.

Candy	School	Horse	Chess	Clouds
Circus	Dogs	Cattle	Corn	Canada
	Monkey		Carpet	

Camping   **Comet**

_____   _____

_____   _____

_____   _____

_____   _____

List the words not found on these encyclopedia pages.

_____   _____   _____

_____   _____   _____

Encyclopedia Unit
Lesson 2

Third Grade Guide Word Worksheet

Use the guide words at the top of the page to help you decide which words would belong on these encyclopedia pages.

Maple Syrup	Mask	Matter	Mantis	Mansion
Mammoth	March	Marble	Maps	Muffin
Monkey	Music	Manatee	Manuscript	

Man

_____

_____

_____

_____

Mars

_____

_____

_____

_____

List the words not found on these encyclopedia pages.

_____ _____ _____

_____ _____ _____

Lesson 3—Classroom

Animal Facts

Objective: Students will extract facts about an animal from a short encyclopedia article.

Science National Standards

NS.K-4.3 LIFE SCIENCE

As a result of activities in grades K–4, all students should develop understanding of

- The characteristics of organisms
- Life cycles of organisms
- Organisms and environments

Skills

- Note taking
- Using guide words
- Identifying an article in a general encyclopedia

Materials

- A copy of a page from an encyclopedia about an animal
- Overhead projector
- Water based markers
- Dry erase board and markers

Instructions

- Make a transparency of the short article. Write questions on the board.

Questions

- What kind of food does this animal eat?
- Where does this animal live?
- What color is this animal?
- What is the size of this animal?
- What enemies does this animal have?

Step 1. Explain to the students that the class will read an article from an encyclopedia to find facts about an animal that will answer the questions on the board.

Step 2. Show the transparency. Find the guide words at the top of the page. Review lesson about guide words. Find the name of the article and note that it is in bold type.

Step 3. Read article together.

Step 4. Tell students they are looking for facts that will answer the questions. (See the instructions for the list of questions.)

Step 5. Circle facts on the transparency.

Step 6. Write facts on the board under the questions.

Teacher's Notes:

Lesson 4—Library/Media Center, Team Teaching

Independent Use of Encyclopedias

Objective: Students will use the encyclopedias to locate information about animals.

Language Arts National Standards

NL-ENG.K-12.3 EVALUATION STRATEGIES

Students apply a wide range of strategies to comprehend, interpret, evaluate, and appreciate texts. They draw on their prior experience, their interactions with other readers and writers, their knowledge of word meaning and of other texts, their word identification strategies, and their understanding of textual features (e.g., sound-letter correspondence, sentence structure, context graphics).

NL-ENG.K-12.12 APPLYING LANGUAGE SKILLS

Students use spoken, written, and visual language to accomplish their own purposes (e.g., for learning, enjoyment, and persuasion, and the exchange of information).

Science National Standards

NS.K-4.3 LIFE SCIENCE

As a result of activities in grades K–4, all students should develop understanding of

- The characteristics of orgasms
- Life cycles of organisms
- Organisms and environments

Skills

- Encyclopedia research
- Fact finding

Materials

- Print fact cards and picture cards on card stock. (Each group will need two sets, one for each game that will be played as outlined in Lesson 5.)
- Encyclopedia sets

- Animals printed on small cards (laminate)
- Animals for word cards:

Apes	Beavers	Camels	Ducks	Elephants
Foxes	Goats	Horses	Kangaroos	Lizards
Monkeys	Owls	Penguins	Rabbits	Snakes
Turtles	Whales			

Step 1. Media Specialist: Review by asking students what they have learned about encyclopedias. Use word cards and overheads from previous lessons if needed for a quick review of how to look up an article.

Step 2. Classroom Teacher: Explain the research plan to the students and brainstorm what facts they might want to find in a general encyclopedia. The teacher can guide students if students have trouble coming up with suggestions.

1. Have students find the article about their animal.

2. Ask students to record the facts on the Fact Cards.

3. Ask students to draw pictures of their animal.

4. Explain that each group will be doing two sets of picture cards and one fact card about their animal to make games that the class will play after all of the research is over.

Step 3. Classroom Teacher: Divide up the students with three or four per group. Allow students to select their animal from the name cards. The classroom teacher can hold cards facing in and fanned out for students to select their animal. Each group should also receive one fact card and also two picture cards.

Step 4. Media Specialist and Classroom Teacher: Rotate and trouble shoot where needed. Collect the finished cards in sets and keep for Lesson 5.

Teacher's Notes:

Fact/Picture Cards

Animal Name

Animal Facts

1. _____

2. _____

3. _____

4. _____

5. _____

6. _____

Picture Card	Picture Card

Lesson 5—Classroom

Animal Games

Objective: Students will identify an animal when given facts. Students will play a memory game with the cards they made in Lesson 4.

Science National Standards

NS.K-4.3 LIFE SCIENCE

As a result of activities in grades K–4, all students should develop understanding of

- The characteristics of organisms
- Life cycles of organisms
- Organisms and environments

Skills

- Animal identification

Materials

- Cards from Lesson 4

What's My Animal?

Step 1. Each group of students takes turns reading their animal facts. The groups read the facts about their animals while the rest of the class tries to guess its name. Students repeat this activity several times to learn the facts about the animal.

Step 2. Continue to share facts until all groups have shared their facts.

Animal Memory Game

Step 1. Using cards from Lesson 4 play a memory game.

Step 2. Lay cards face down on the floor. Students sit in a circle around the cards.

Step 3. Take turns turning over cards to find matches. Because of the small number of cards, each person receives one turn even if they find a match.

Optional Activity: Students may play game during free time or as a reward for finished work.

Resources

New Book of Knowledge. Danbury, Conn.: Grolier, 2002.

Rourke's World of Science Encyclopedia. Vero Beach, Fla.: Rourke, 1999.

World Book Student Discovery Encyclopedia. Chicago: World Book, 2000.

Part Three

Almanac
Unit

Lesson 1—Library/Media Center, Team Teaching

Introduction

Objective: Students will determine the types of information found in an almanac.

Language Arts National Standards

NL-ENG.K-12.3 EVALUATION STRATEGIES

Students apply a wide range of strategies to comprehend, interpret, evaluate, and appreciate texts. They draw on their prior experience, their interactions with other readers and writers, their knowledge of word meaning and of other texts, their word identification strategies, and their understanding of textual features (e.g., sound-letter correspondence, sentence structure, context graphics).

NL-ENG.K-12.12 APPLYING LANGUAGE SKILLS

Students use spoken, written, and visual language to accomplish their own purposes (e.g., for learning, enjoyment, and persuasion, and the exchange of information).

Skills

- Almanac research
- Fact finding

Materials

- Favorite topic worksheet for each group
- Set of student almanacs (*The World Almanac for Kids*. Mahwah, N.J.: World Almanac Books, 2003)
- Overhead projector and transparency
- Definition and call number cards enlarged and laminated

Step 1. Media Specialist: As the students enter the library/media center, seat them around the reference section where almanacs are located.

Step 2. Media Specialist: Using the definition and call number cards, explain that the items in this group of reference works are printed each year and contain information about facts and figures related to everyday life. Point out several of the articles that will interest the students. The movie section is a favorite.

Step 3. Classroom Teacher: Give out the almanacs to groups of students. The size of the groups will depend on the number of almanacs in the collection. Smaller groups of two or three are best. Allow time for students to page through and discover facts and topics found in the books. Ask students to look for a favorite topic that is in the almanac. Each group will need to complete the sentence page on favorite topics. (See worksheet.) Read through the worksheet together and break up students into small groups so that they have space to work and complete the worksheet.

Step 4. Classroom Teacher: Set up the overhead projector and bring the students back to together as a large group for sharing time.

Step 5. Media Specialist: As students share, write what they found on the puffy clouds of the overhead. Summarize by completing the statement at the bottom of the sheet.

Step 6. Media Specialist: Collect group papers and arrange in a booklet or post on the board.

Teacher's Notes:

Word and Definition Cards

Cut, enlarge, and paste onto construction paper.

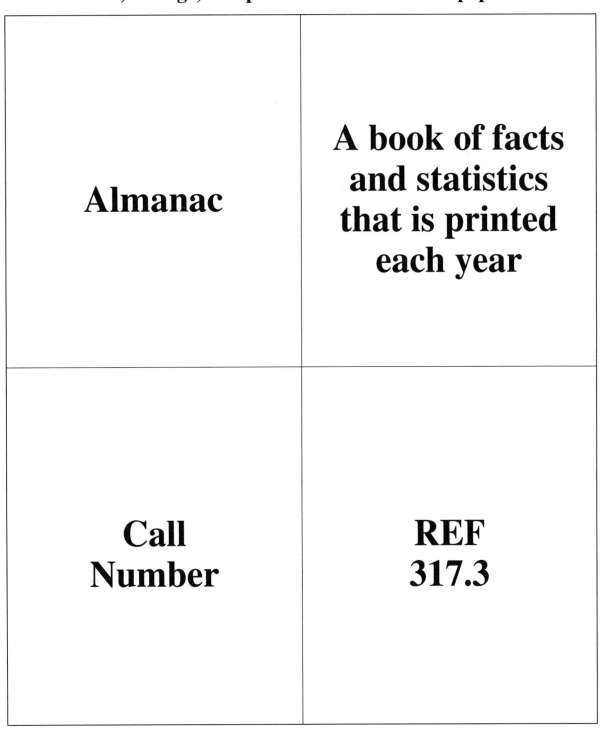

Almanac

A book of facts and statistics that is printed each year

Call Number

REF 317.3

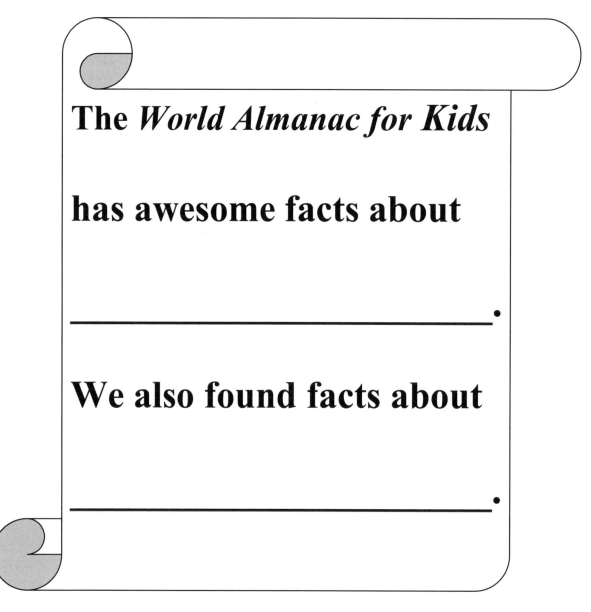

The *World Almanac for Kids*

has awesome facts about

_____ .

We also found facts about

_____ .

Students in our group:

_____

_____

Summary
Most of our almanac information was

_____

_____

_____

_____

Lesson 2—Classroom, Team Teaching

Table of Contents and Index

Objective: Students will understand the terms "table of contents" and "index."

Language Arts National Standards

NL-ENG.K-12.3N EVALUATION STRATEGIES

Students apply a wide range of strategies to comprehend, interpret, evaluate, and appreciate texts. They draw on their prior experience, their interactions with other readers and writers, their knowledge of word meaning and of other texts, their word identification strategies, and their understanding of textual features (e.g., sound-letter correspondence, sentence structure, context graphics).

NL-ENG.K-12.12 APPLYING LANGUAGE SKILLS

Students use spoken, written, and visual language to accomplish their own purposes (e.g., for learning, enjoyment, and persuasion, and the exchange of information).

Skills

- Using a table of contents
- Using an index

Materials

- Student almanacs (*The World Almanac for Kids*. Mahwah, N.J.: World Almanac Books, 2003)
- Word and definition cards for table of contents and index

Step 1. Media Specialist: Introduce the terms "table of contents" and "index." Show word cards and discuss definitions. Tell students that a table of contents is a list of the chapters and page numbers found in a book. The index, an alphabetic list of subjects, is found at the end of a book.

Step 2. Classroom Teacher: Pass out the almanacs to each student or small groups of students depending on how many almanacs you have. Look at the table of contents. Discuss the first section, "Faces and Places." Look at the articles under "Faces and Places." Draw students' attention to the article, "Birthdays of Celebrities" and discuss. Find the page of a chosen subject and turn to the article. Allow students time to explore this page.

Step 3. Classroom Teacher: Ask several students to find and then tell the class the birthday of an interesting person.

Step 4. Media Specialist: Look at the index to find "Birthdays of Celebrities." Find the correct page for this in the index. Ask students to try finding names of individual celebrities from Step 3. Looking at the index, the students will realize that they cannot look up individual names in the "Birthdays of Celebrities." Have students turn to the table of contents and look again at "Birthdays of Celebrities." Students will notice that they cannot lookup individual names from the "Birthdays of Celebrities" listing in the table of contents. Tell the students that sometimes they will need to look in a different place for information.

Step 5. Classroom Teacher: Divide the class into groups. Each group will explore an article in one section of the table contents. The group will look up the article using the table of contents and index. Students will complete the worksheet.

Step 6. Share information.

Teacher's Notes:

Almanac
Table of Contents and Index

Names of people in group

What is the name of the section in the table of contents the group is looking up?

What is the name and page number of the article the group is looking up?

What is the name and page number of the article in the index the group is looking up?

What information did the group find?

Lesson 3—Almanac Unit, Library/Media Center, Team Teaching

Fact Finding

Objective: Students will find facts in the almanac using the table of contents and the index.

Language Arts National Standards

NL-ENG.K-12.3 EVALUATION STRATEGIES

Students apply a wide range of strategies to comprehend, interpret, evaluate, and appreciate texts. They draw on their prior experience, their interactions with other readers and writers, their knowledge of word meaning and of other texts, their word identification strategies, and their understanding of textual features (e.g., sound-letter correspondence, sentence structure, context graphics).

NL-ENG.K-12.12 APPLYING LANGUAGE SKILLS

Students use spoken, written, and visual language to accomplish their own purposes (e.g., for learning, enjoyment, and persuasion, and the exchange of information).

Skills

- Almanac research
- Fact finding

Materials

- Worksheet of finding facts
- Collection of student almanacs
- Overhead transparency from Lesson 1
- Definition and call number cards from Lesson 1

Step 1. Media Specialist: Review the basic information covered in Lessons 1 and 2. Review both the definition of an almanac and the steps to finding information using the index and the table of contents.

Step 2. Classroom Teacher: Model finding a fact in the almanac. Example: How many one dollar bills are in circulation?

Step 3. Classroom Teacher: Third grade students—Pair up students depending on the number of almanacs available. Go over the directions for completing the worksheet and let students work independently. Second grade students—The classroom teacher will make an overhead transparency of the worksheet. The classroom teacher and students then work together to complete the worksheet.

Step 4. Media Specialist: Gather students back together in the large group and review by checking the information that the students found.

Closure. Students should circle the most interesting fact on their worksheet.

Answers to the Worksheet

Second Grade	Third Grade
1. b	1. b
2. a	2. a
3. c	3. c
4. c	4. c
	5. b
	6. Sahara, Africa

Teacher's Notes:

Use the almanac to check for the correct information. Circle the letter on your page that answers the question.

1. What is the tallest building in the United States?
    a. Chrysler Building
    b. Sears Tower
    c. John Hancock Center

2. Who was the 30th president of the United States?
    a. Calvin Coolidge
    b. Jimmy Carter
    c. John Tyler

3. What is the largest animal in the world?
    a. elephant
    b. crocodile
    c. blue whale

4. The first modern Olympic game was held in what year?
    a. 1928
    b. 1994
    c. 1896

Third Grade Worksheet

Use the almanac to check for the correct information.

1. What is the tallest building in the United States?
    a. Chrysler Building
    b. Sears Tower
    c. John Hancock Center

2. Who was the 30th president of the United States?
    a. Calvin Coolidge
    b. Jimmy Carter
    c. John Tyler

3. What is the largest animal in the world?
    a. elephant
    b. crocodile
    c. blue whale

4. The first modern Olympic game was held in what year?
    a. 1928
    b. 1994
    c. 1896

5. What is the largest city (most people) in the world?
    a. Calcutta
    b. Tokyo
    c. New York

    Where is it located?

Lesson 4—Classroom

Writing Questions

Objective: Students will find favorite facts in the almanac and write questions relating to those facts.

Language Arts National Standards

NL-ENG.K-12.3 EVALUATION STRATEGIES

Students apply a wide range of strategies to comprehend, interpret, evaluate, and appreciate texts. They draw on their prior experience, their interactions with other readers and writers, their knowledge of word meaning and of other texts, their word identification strategies, and their understanding of textual features (e.g., sound-letter correspondence, sentence structure, context graphics).

NL-ENG.K-12.12 APPLYING LANGUAGE SKILLS

Students use spoken, written, and visual language to accomplish their own purposes (e.g., for learning, enjoyment, persuasion, and the exchange of information).

Materials

- Almanacs (*The World Almanac for Kids*. Mahwah, N.J.: World Almanac Books, 2003)
- Worksheet copied for each student
- Pencils

Step 1. Classroom Teacher: Show examples of questions. (When is Britney Spears's birthday? Who was the first president of the United States?) Tell students they are going to write questions for a game.

Step 2. Explain to students that they need to include the question, answer, and page number where answer is found.

Step 3. Pass out almanacs and find answers to the sample questions. Stress the process of using the table of contents and index.

Step 4. Pass out the worksheet and explain the activity.

Step 5. Students complete activity.

Teacher's Notes:

Question _____

_____

_____

Answer _____

_____

_____

Page Number _____

Question _____

_____

_____

Answer _____

_____

_____

Page Number _____

Lesson 5—Classroom

Almanac Drill

Objective: Students will play the game Almanac Drill to learn how to use the table of contents and index to find information in the almanac.

Language Arts National Standards

NL-ENG.K-12.3 EVALUATION STRATEGIES

Students apply a wide range of strategies to comprehend, interpret, evaluate, and appreciate texts. They draw on their prior experience, their interactions with other readers and writers, their knowledge of word meaning and of other texts, their word identification strategies, and their understanding of textual features (e.g., sound-letter correspondence, sentence structure, context graphics).

NL-ENG.K-12.12 APPLYING LANGUAGE SKILLS

Students use spoken, written, and visual language to accomplish their own purposes (e.g., for learning, enjoyment, and persuasion, and the exchange of information).

Materials

- Almanacs
- Questions from Lesson 4
- Markers and dry erase board
- Rewards (e.g., extra computer time, pencils, bookmarks)

Step 1. Divide class into two teams. Write teams' names on the board for score keeping.

Step 2. Pass out almanacs, one for each student.

Step 3. Explain game: The classroom teacher will read a question. After the question is read, the classroom teacher will say, "Go." Students will try to find the page number and answer using the table of contents and index. When a student finds the page number and answer, he or she stands and waits for the classroom teacher to call on the first student standing. The student reads the answer and page number. If answer is correct, give one point for that team.

Step 4. Play game for 30 minutes or until all questions are answered.

Step 5. Reward winning team.

Teacher's Notes:

Resource Page

Books

The World Almanac for Kids. Mahwah, N.J.: World Almanac Books, 2003.

Web Sites

http://www.worldalmanacforkids.com

Part Four

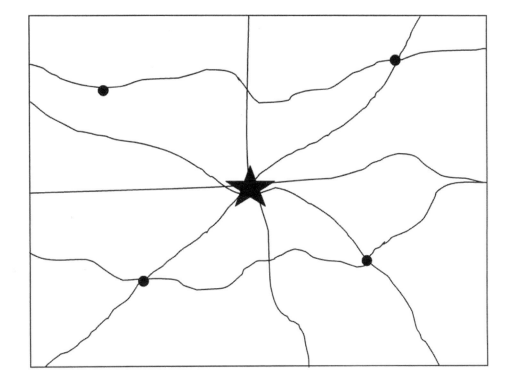

Atlas
Unit

Lesson 1—Classroom

Summer Vacations

Objective: Teacher and students will share their summer vacation travels, while locating destinations and coloring destinations on a map of the United States.

Geography National Standards

NSS-G.K-12.1 THE WORLD IN SPATIAL TERMS

As a result of activities in grades K–12, all students should understand how to use maps and other geographic representations, tools, and technologies to acquire, process, and report information from a spatial perspective.

Skill

- Map skills
- Location of states

Materials

- Maps of states where teacher has traveled
- Pictures of teacher's summer vacation
- Die cut of a car similar to teacher's
- Copies of U.S. map for each student (for a map, visit http://www.eduplace.com/ss/maps/pdf/uscap.pdf)
- Crayons
- Transparency of U.S. map
- Overhead projector
- Colored water-based markers

Preparation of Materials

- Visit Web site above to print U.S. map. Copy map one per student.
- Make a transparency of the U.S. map.

Step 1. The classroom teacher uses state maps, pictures, and die cut of car to tell about his or her summer vacation. Display the map on a bulletin board or easel. Trace the route taken on the map, moving the car along the roads and stopping for important activities. Show pictures as needed.

Step 2. Pass out U.S. maps to students.

Step 3. Each student is allowed to share one place they traveled to over the summer. As students share, the class colors in the appropriate states. The students color only the states where the class has traveled.

Closure. After everyone has shared, the class composes a sentence to describe the completed map. Example: Mrs. Jones's class traveled to these states this past summer. Write the sentence on bottom of map.

Optional Activity: Using the worksheet, have students graph the states they have visited.

Teacher's Notes:

Atlas Unit
Lesson 1

Graphing Worksheet

Ohio	**Kentucky**	**Indiana**	**Michigan**	**Pennsylvania**

Lesson 2—Library/Media Center, Team Teaching

Discovering an Atlas

Objective: Students will learn the way an atlas is used and where atlases are located in the library/media center. Students will also practice using the legend or key from a road map and locate special places.

Geography National Standards

NSS-G.K-12.1 THE WORLD IN SPATIAL TERMS

As a result of activities in grades K–12, all students should understand how to use maps and other geographic representations, tools, and technologies to acquire, process, and report information from a spatial perspective.

Skills

- Map Skills

Materials

- Different types of atlases, both student and general use
- Word cards for atlas, legend, and call number (see worksheet)
- Road atlases for several small groups
- Worksheet about legend or key symbols

Step 1. Media Specialist: Greet students and seat them around you in the reference section where the atlas collection is located. Talk to the students about the reference section. Use the word card with the call number of the atlas collection to reinforce that this call number is different from the call number of the other nonfiction section (e.g., REF stands for "reference"). Show several kinds of atlases depending on your collection.

Step 2. Classroom Teacher: Use the word cards to explain the definition of an atlas. Share some basic features as you page through an atlas from the library/media collection. Stress the table of contents, introductory pages, individual country and state pages, index, and glossary.

Step 3. Classroom Teacher: Introduce the definition of "key" or "legend" using the word cards that have been prepared ahead of time. Use a road map and share with students how the pictures or symbols make it easier to read.

Step 4. Media Specialist: Divide the class into small groups. Explain the group work. Write the steps on the board so that students can refer to them during the group time.

1. Find the key on a map in the road atlas.

2. Pick out three symbols and locate those items on the map.

3. Match up the symbols on the worksheet to the correct term name. Students can use the map as resource if needed.

4. Follow the directions for coloring of the symbols as stated on the worksheet.

The media specialist and classroom teacher rotate around the room to help where needed.

Closure. Classroom Teacher: Review the word cards by hiding the definitions of atlas, legend, and call number. Ask students to give the correct word.

Teacher's Notes:

Word and Definition Cards

Cut, enlarge, and paste onto construction paper.

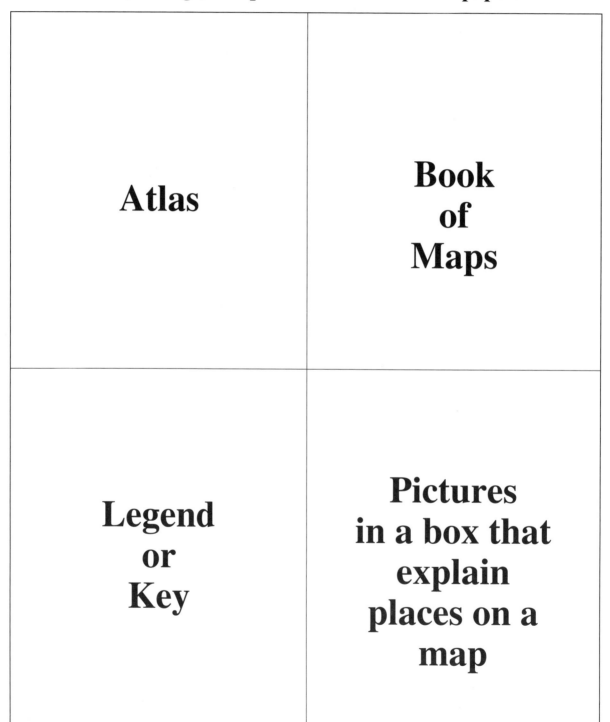

Atlas	**Book of Maps**
Legend or Key	**Pictures in a box that explain places on a map**

Word and Definition Cards

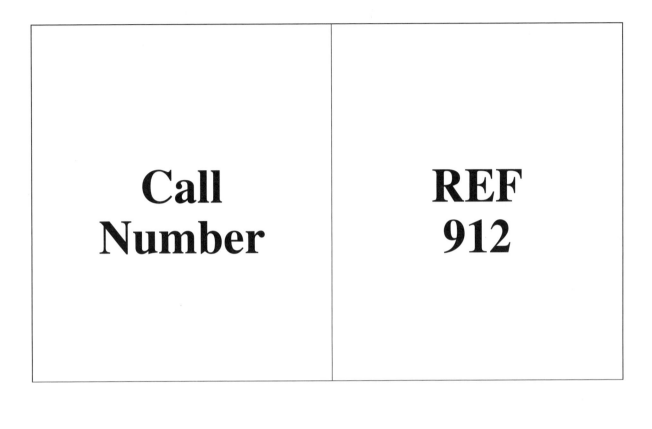

| Call Number | REF 912 |

Second Grade Legend Worksheet

Match up the symbols with the correct name on the right-hand side of the page. Follow the directions for coloring the symbols.

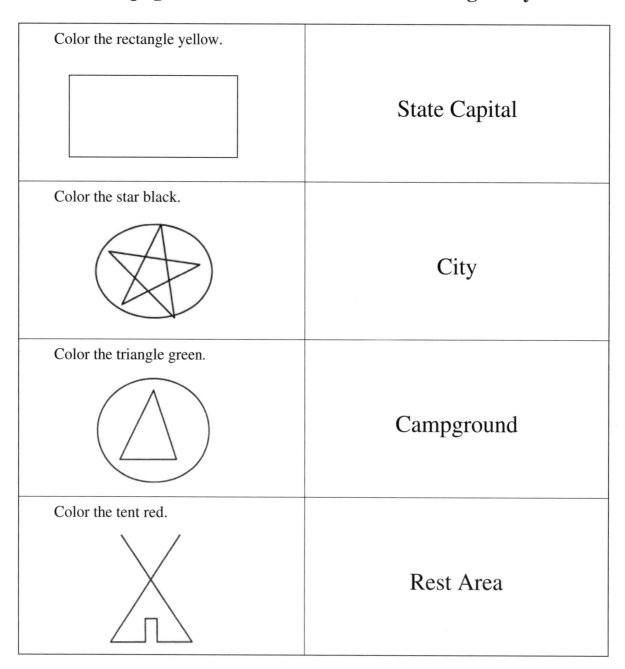

Color the rectangle yellow.	State Capital
Color the star black.	City
Color the triangle green.	Campground
Color the tent red.	Rest Area

A small black airplane is the symbol for a passenger service airport. Draw one on the back of this paper.

Third Grade Legend Worksheet

Match up the symbols with the correct name on the right-hand side of the page. Follow the directions for coloring the symbols.

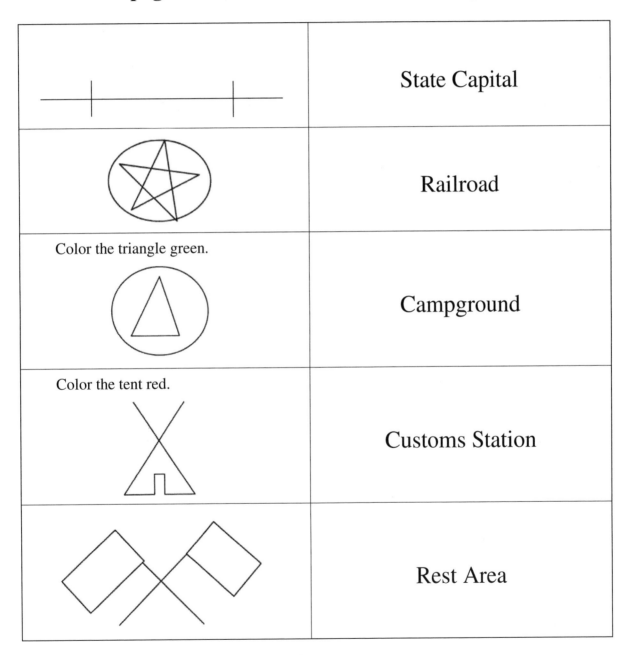

	State Capital
	Railroad
Color the triangle green.	Campground
Color the tent red.	Customs Station
	Rest Area

A small black airplane is the symbol for a passenger service airport. Draw one on the back of this paper. Where would you go if you were flying on an airplane? Use a complete sentence to describe where you would fly.

Lesson 3—Classroom

State Puzzles

Objective: Students will put together state puzzles and use the legend or key symbols to find items on the maps.

Geography National Standards

NSS-G.K-12.1 THE WORLD IN SPATIAL TERMS

As a result of activities in grades K–12, all students should understand how to use maps and other geographic representations, tools, and technologies to acquire, process, and report information from a spatial perspective.

Skills

- Map skills
- Legend or key

Materials

- State maps from an old road atlas
- Construction paper
- Rubber cement
- Worksheet copied for each group
- Large envelopes to store puzzles
- Key or legend from the road atlas enlarged for easy viewing

Preparation of Materials

- Cut out state maps. Glue maps onto construction paper and write the name of the state on construction paper. Laminate maps. Cut the maps up into puzzles and give each state a number. Write that number on the backs of the pieces of the puzzle. Place puzzle pieces in an envelope.

Step 1. Review the concept of key or legend from the previous lesson. Show the enlarged key or legend. Tell students they will be looking for the items from the legend or key on the puzzle maps.

Step 2. Divide the class into groups of two or three students. Give each group a puzzle map and a worksheet.

Step 3. Explain the activity. Students will assemble the maps and then use the maps to answer the questions on the worksheet.

Step 4. Students will share information about their state puzzle maps.

State Puzzle Worksheet

1. What is the name of your state?

   _____

2. What is the name of the state capital?

   _____

3. What is the name of a historical site?

   _____

4. What is the name of an airport?

   _____

5. What is the name of a park?

   _____

6. What is the name of a town that is not the state capital?

   _____

7. What is the name of a hospital?

   _____

8. What is the name of a campground?

   _____

9. What is the name of a main interstate road?

   _____

10. What is the name of a lake?

    _____

11. What is the name of a river?

    _____

Lesson 4—Library/Media Center, Team Teaching

Longitude, Latitude, and Key Locators

Objective: Students will be able to plot points on a road map using longitudinal and latitudinal measurements.

Geography National Standards

NSS-G.K-12.1 THE WORLD IN SPATIAL TERMS

Understand how to use maps and other geographic representations, tools, and technologies to acquire, process, and report information from a spatial perspective.

Skills

- Map Skills

Materials

- Word cards for longitude and latitude. (See worksheet.)
- Word cards for terms covered in Lesson 2
- Road atlases for several small groups used in Lesson 2
- Worksheet on map index
- Yarn (two pieces for each group, about 18 inches long)
- Enlarged section of the index found on a state map in a road atlas and reproduced as an overhead. The section to be enlarged should be after the towns and cities listings (places of interest).
- Blank overhead
- A state map

Step 1. Media Specialist: Review from Lesson 2 the words and definitions for atlas, legend, and call number.

Step 2. Classroom Teacher: Introduce word cards for longitude and latitude and explain how we locate places on a map in an atlas using the coordinates listed in the index. Model locating your hometown in state using the yarn. One piece of yarn is for the longitude and the other piece for the latitude. First, find it listed in the index and then use the longitude and latitude to locate it on the state map. Ask a student to help locate the hometown. The student can be the longitude, and the classroom teacher can be the latitude. Where the yarn crosses is the location of the hometown. Longitude and latitude are not used on a road atlas; instead key locator terms are listed in the index (e.g., "F6").

Step 3. Media Specialist: Use the overhead of the index, show where the places of interest are listed. Example: Military Facilities—name—coordinates. Write this out on a blank overhead for students to refer to when they do the worksheet.

Step 4. Classroom Teacher: Divide the class into small groups and go over the group work and worksheet on map indexing.

1. Each group will practice finding a city or town listed in the index using the maps and yarn that has been provided. The state capital would be a place to start. The state capital can be listed on the board or copied and handed out with the road maps. These will depend on the state maps you are using.

2. Complete the worksheet. Review the places of interest that was covered in step 3. Classroom teacher and media specialist will rotate around the room helping where needed.

Closure. Students that finish early can look for their hometown in a world atlas. Lay these out ahead of time for this purpose.

Teacher's Notes:

Word and Definition Cards

Cut, enlarge, and paste onto construction paper.

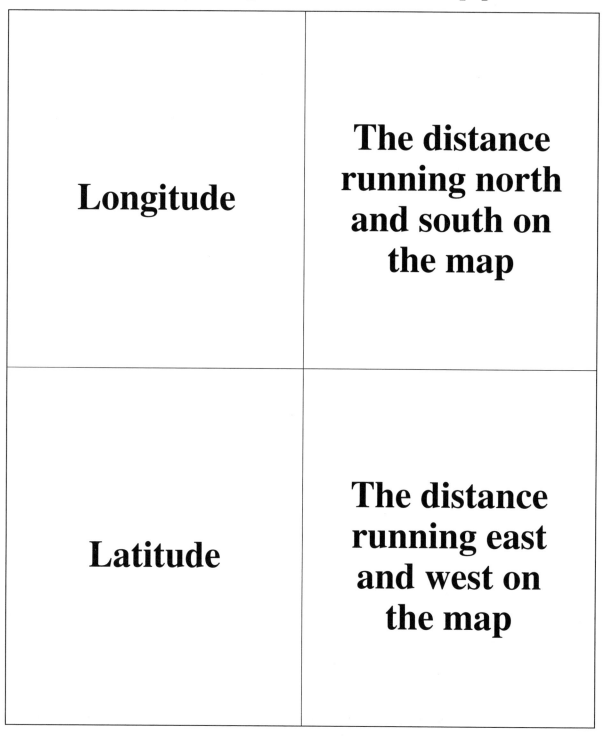

| **Longitude** | **The distance running north and south on the map** |
| **Latitude** | **The distance running east and west on the map** |

Atlas Unit
Lesson 4

Second Grade Map Index Worksheet

Find the index section on your road map and fill in the blank spaces with the correct name and map key locators. Use a section of yarn to help in the plotting of those key locators.

Names of students in your group_____

_____

_____

_____

_____

1. The name of the state our group is working with is _____.

2. What are the map key locators for the state capital? _____.

3. What are the map key locators and name for a lake?

    Name_____ Map coordinates_____

4. What are the map key locators and name for a national/state park and forest?

    Name_____ Map coordinates_____

5. What are the map key locators and name of a principal place of interest?

    Name_____ Map coordinates_____

Atlas Unit
Lesson 4

Third Grade Map Index Worksheet

Find the index section on your road map and fill in the blank spaces with the correct name and map key locators. Use a section of yarn to help in the plotting of those key locators.

Names of students in your group_____

_____

_____

_____

_____

1. The name of the state our group is working with is _____.

2. What are the map key locators for the state capital? _____.

3. What are the map key locators and name for a lake?

    Name_____ Map coordinates_____

4. What are the map key locators and name for a national/state park and forest?

    Name_____ Map coordinates_____

5. What are the map key locators and name of a principal place of interest?

    Name_____ Map coordinates_____

6. What are the map key locators and name for an airport?

    Name_____ Map coordinates_____

7. What are the map key locators and name of military facilities?

    Name_____ Map coordinates_____

Lesson 5—Classroom, Team Teaching

Making an Atlas

Objective: Students will make a school atlas.

Geography National Standards

NSS-G.K-12.1 THE WORLD IN SPATIAL TERMS

As a result of activities in grades K–12, all students should understand how to use maps and other geographic representations, tools, and technologies to acquire, process, and report information from a spatial perspective.

Skills

- Map Skills

Materials

- Word cards from previous lessons
- Dry eraser board and markers
- Patterns prepared
- Two copies of the worksheet for each group

Preparing the materials: Trace, cutout, and laminate patterns to represent the items in the classroom.

Step 1. Using word cards, the classroom teacher reviews maps, keys, and legends. Media specialist reviews the atlas by showing examples of the title page, dedication page, index, and glossary. Place pattern pieces on the board arranging them in their proper places. Make a key or legend with markers in the corner of the map.

Step 2. Divide the class into six groups. Assign a different room in the school to each group.

Step 3. Explain to students that they will be making a map, key, or legend of a room (library/media center, music room, cafeteria, gym, art room, or principal's office) in the school using the worksheet. Each group will also be completing an additional page in the atlas (cover, dedication page, table of contents, glossary, or index).

Step 4. Classroom teacher accompanies three groups to rooms and the media specialist goes with the other three groups.

Step 5. Students will observe the layout of the rooms and make notes on one worksheet. This worksheet will be their sloppy copy.

Step 6. Students will return to the classroom to complete their map on the second worksheet.

Step 7. Students will complete the additional page for the atlas.

Step 8. Bind atlas into a book and place in the library/media center for circulation.

Pattern

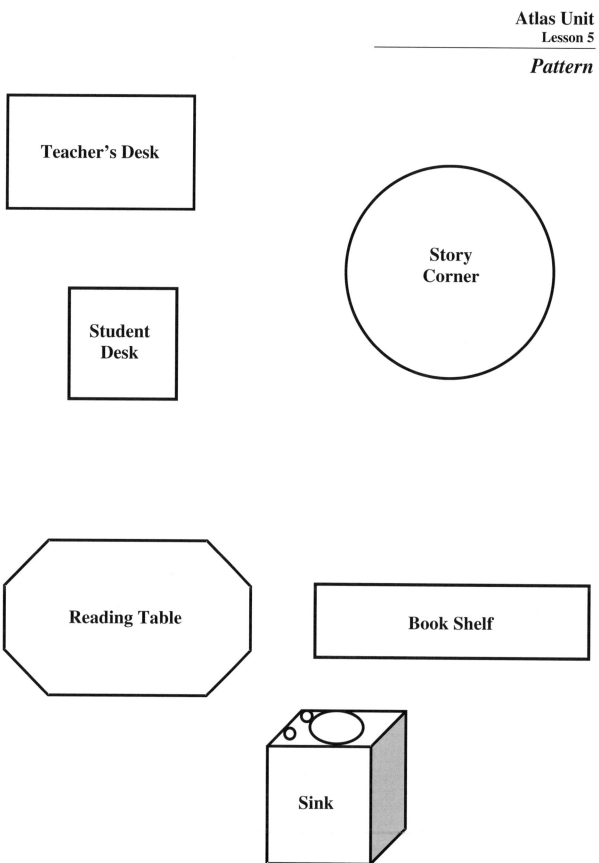

Teacher's Desk

Story
Corner

Student
Desk

Reading Table

Book Shelf

Sink

Pattern

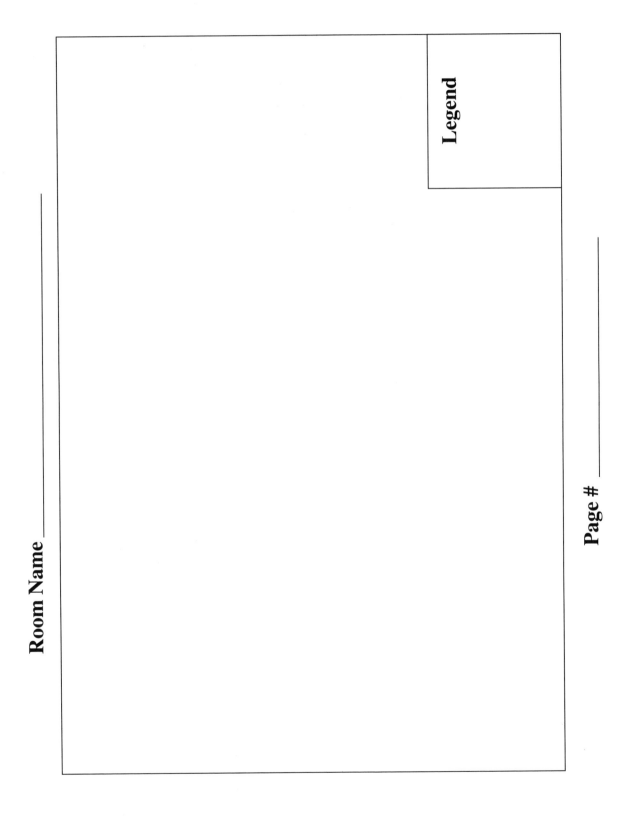

Resources

Books

Children's Atlas. New York: Facts on File, 2000.

Geography for Life. Collingdale, Penn.: Diane Publishing, 1994.

Lye, Keith. *The New Children's Illustrated Atlas of the World.* Philadelphia: Courage Books, 1999.

The New Millennium Atlas of the United States, Canada and the World. Milwaukee, Wisc.: Gareth Stevens, 2000.

Rubel, David. *Scholastic Atlas of the United States.* New York: Scholastic, 2000.

Steele, Philip. *Scholastic Atlas of the World.* New York: Scholastic, 2001.

Web Sites

http://www.eduplace.com/ss/maps/pdf/uscap.pdf

Part Five

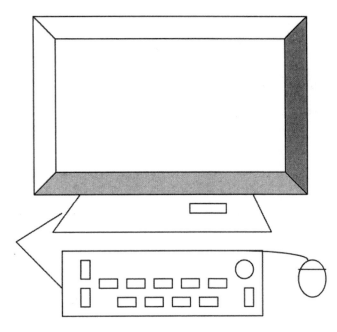

Online Catalog
Unit

Note: Our Online Catalog Unit is an essential part of today's library/media center curriculum. The first three lessons in this unit need to be taught by the media specialist, but the last three can utilize the classroom teacher and fit into any curricular unit. We have found that the team-teaching approach reinforces and strengthens both the library/media center skills and the classroom curriculum.

Lesson 1—Library/Media Center

Subject Headings

Objective: Students will use the online catalog system to locate a book using the subject heading on the computer.

Language Arts National Standards

NL-ENG.K-12.4 COMMUNICATION SKILLS

Students adjust their use of spoken, written, and visual language (e.g., conventions, style, vocabulary) to communicate effectively with a variety of audiences and for different purposes.

NL-ENG.K-12.6 APPLYING KNOWLEDGE

Students apply knowledge of language structure, language conventions (e.g., spelling and punctuation), media techniques, figurative language, and genre to create, critique, and discuss print and nonprint texts.

NL-ENG.K-12.12 APPLYING LANGUAGE SKILLS

Students use spoken, written, and visual language to accomplish their own purposes (e.g., for learning, enjoyment, persuasion, and the exchange of information).

Skills

- Typing
- Searching the online catalog

Materials

- Word card and definition for subject (see word card page; enlarge and laminate)
- Overhead of subject web
- Copies of subject worksheet

Step 1. Introduce the unit by explaining that students don't have to remember whether the library/media center has a specific book, magazine, or reference material. The computer stores all the titles and authors, and we can easily check to see if a book is in our library/media center.

Step 2. Use the definition card for subject (e.g., cats, dogs, hamsters) and go over its meaning and how it relates to using the online catalog system. Stress that all of the books and materials in the library/media center are listed under different subject headings, and this makes it easier for us to locate what we need.

Step 3. Use the overhead subject web to brainstorm different types of pets. Explain to the students how we need to tell the computer exactly what we want to look up. The computer does all of the work and gives us a list of resources.

Step 4—Computer time. Work with groups of students depending on the number of computers in your station setup. The remaining students can do the subject word search worksheet. Alternate the groups until all of the students have had an opportunity to work through the following steps:

1. Type in a subject. (It's best if the whole group uses the same subject on the first practice time. A later lesson gives the students the freedom to choose a subject on their own.)

2. Click on the subject icon.

3. Highlight the subject and number of books available.

4. Click on "Select."

5. Check the following: title, author, call number, and status (in/checked out).

6. Close out each screen.

Teacher's Notes:

Subject

A main topic you want to read about or research

Subject Worksheet

```
P   F   I   S   H   N   B   O   C   A
L   D   R   I   B   C   T   E   V   I
I   B   O   A   T   A   K   C   O   R
R   S   D   V   A   T   H   V   T   P
F   O   O   T   B   A   L   L   K   L
N   C   G   Y   J   A   I   F   S   A
C   C   V   B   I   J   T   E   S   N
U   E   S   N   A   K   E   N   W   E
T   R   A   I   N   E   B   T   O   Z
H   A   M   S   T   E   R   Y   C   T
```

AIRPLANE	TRAIN	COW	ROCK
SOCCER	HAMSTER	FOOTBALL	BIRD
BAT	BOAT	FISH	SNAKE
CAT			

I would like to read books about_____

_____

_____.

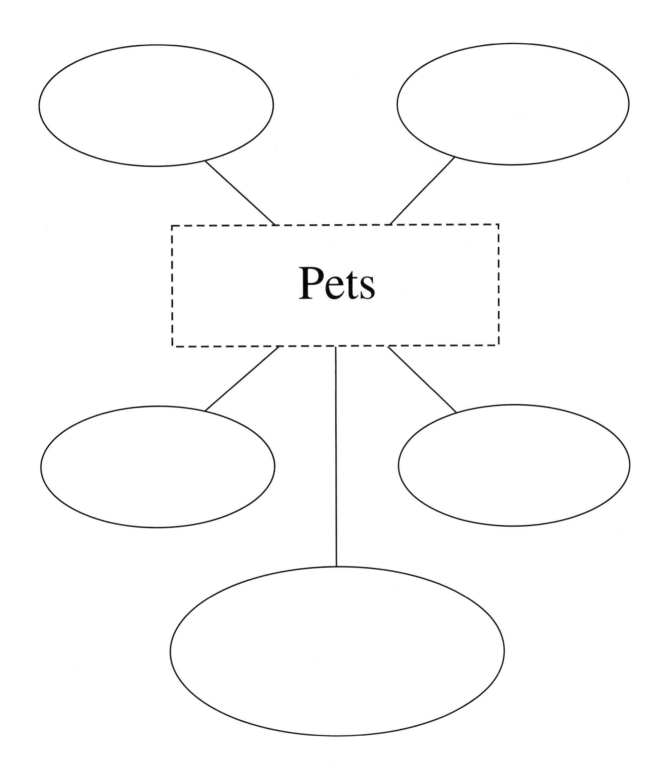

Lesson 2—Library/Media Center

Title Headings

Objective: Students use the online catalog system to locate a book using the title heading on the computer.

Language Arts National Standards

NL-ENG.K-12.4 COMMUNICATION SKILLS

Students adjust their use of spoken, written, and visual language (e.g., conventions, style, vocabulary) to communicate effectively with a variety of audiences and for different purposes.

NL-ENG.K-12.6 APPLYING KNOWLEDGE

Students apply knowledge of language structure, language conventions (e.g., spelling and punctuation), media techniques, figurative language, and genre to create, critique, and discuss print and nonprint texts.

NL-ENG.K-12.12 APPLYING LANGUAGE SKILLS

Students use spoken, written, and visual language to accomplish their own purposes (e.g., for learning, enjoyment, persuasion, and the exchange of information).

Skills

- Typing
- Searching the online catalog

Materials

- Word card and definition for title (see word card page; enlarge and laminate)
- Copies of title worksheet

Step 1. Review Lesson 1 by asking key questions. Examples:

How did we look up a book last week?

What did we type into the computer first?

Give an example of a subject.

Step 2. Using the title definition card, go over the meaning of the title and how it relates to using the online catalog system. Stress that all of the books and materials in the library/media center are listed by titles. Example: *Clifford: The Big Red Dog*

Step 3—Computer time. Work with small groups of students depending on the number of computers in your station setup. The remaining students can do the title worksheet. Alternate the groups until the media specialist has guided all of the students through the following steps:

1. Type in a book title (it's best if the whole group uses the same title on the first practice time). A later lesson gives the students the freedom to choose subjects on their own.
    Examples:

    Clifford at the Circus

    Rainbow Fish

2. Click on the title icon (title will appear highlighted).

3. Check the following: title, author, call number, and status (in/checked out).

4. Close out each screen.

5. Practice with a second title if time permits (*Green Eggs and Ham*).

Teacher's Notes:

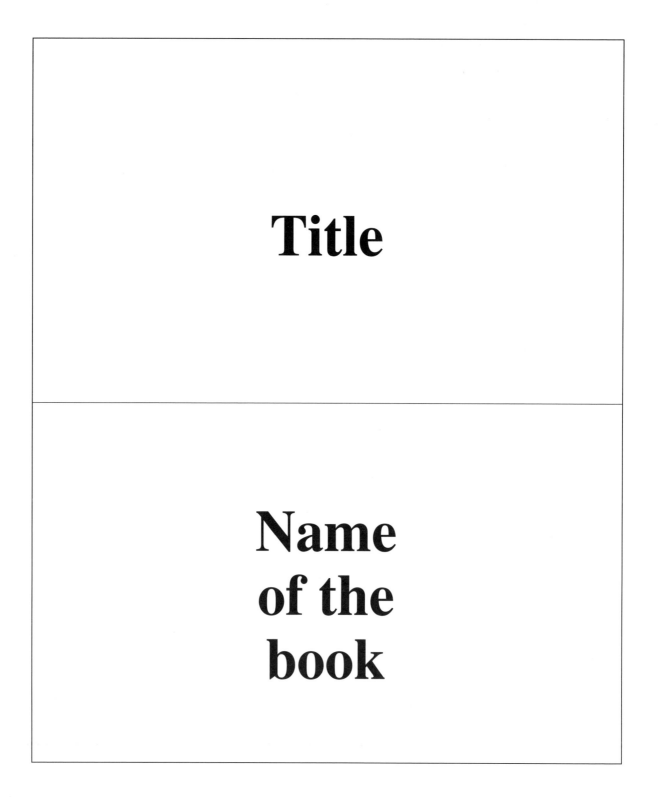

Title Worksheet

Underline the titles of the books on this page and circle the names of the authors.

David Shannon   Pilots Fly Planes

Green Eggs and Ham   Dr. Seuss

Rainbow Fish   Cynthia Rylant

The Three Little Pigs   Hurricanes

Jan Brett   Lives of Insects

No, David!   Mary Pope Osborne

Snowed in at Pokeweed Public School

Firefighters Fight Fires

Put a star by the title of the books you would like to read.

Lesson 3—Library/Media Center

Author Headings

Objective: Students will use the online catalog system to locate a book using the author heading on the computer.

Language Arts National Standards

NL-ENG.K-12.4 COMMUNICATION SKILLS

Students adjust their use of spoken, written, and visual language (e.g., conventions, style, vocabulary) to communicate effectively with a variety of audiences and for different purposes.

NL-ENG.K-12.6 APPLYING KNOWLEDGE

Students apply knowledge of language structure, language conventions (e.g., spelling and punctuation), media techniques, figurative language, and genre to create, critique, and discuss print and nonprint texts.

NL-ENG.K-12.12 APPLYING LANGUAGE SKILLS

Students use spoken, written, and visual language to accomplish their own purposes (e.g., for learning, enjoyment, persuasion, and the exchange of information).

Skills

- Typing
- Searching the online catalog

Materials

- Word card and definition for author (see word card page; enlarge and laminate)
- Copies of author worksheet

Step 1. Review the process of looking up books on the computer covered in the previous lessons. Examples of questions to ask students:

How did we look up a book last week?

What did we type into the computer first?

Step 2. Using the definition card for author, go over how the meaning relates to using the online catalog system. Stress that all of the books and materials in the library/media center are listed by the authors last name. Each author is listed by last name, first name, and then middle. Example: Mary Pope Osborne—Osborne, Mary Pope

Step 3—Computer time. Work with small groups of students depending on the number of computers in your station setup. The remaining students can do the author worksheet. Go over the directions for the worksheet before breaking into computer groups. Alternate the groups until the media specialist has guided all of the students through the following steps:

1. Type in the author's name: last name—comma—space—first name—space—middle name or initial. Example: Mary Pope Osborne (it's best if the whole group uses the same title on the first practice time). A later lesson gives the students the freedom to choose a subject on their own.

2. Click on the author icon (the author's name and the number of books will be highlighted).

3. Click "Select," and all the titles of books by this author will appear on the screen. Point out that these are the books in your system. This author may have written more, but if the library system doesn't have the books, they would not be listed on screen.

4. Page down through the titles and pick one that you wish to read. Check the status of the book. Ask students to identify the call number you would need to locate this book on the shelf. Close out each screen.

5. Practice with a second author if time permits. Example: Dr. Seuss

Teacher's Notes:

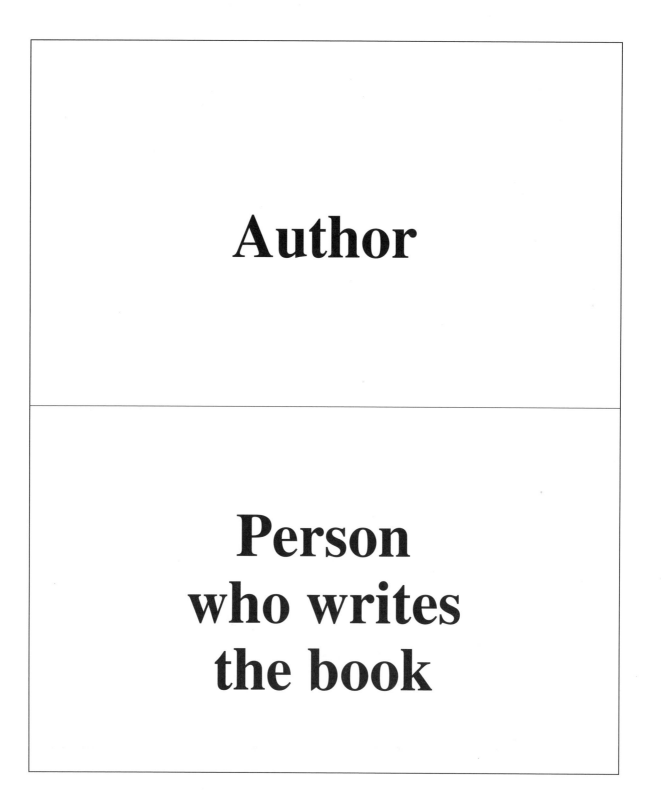

Online Catalog Unit
Lesson 3

Author Worksheet

Rewrite the authors' names as you would need to type them into the online catalog program.

(last name comma space first name space middle name)

Eric Carle   Carle, Eric

Marc Brown_____

David Adler_____

Debbie Dadey_____

Barbara Park_____

Jan Brett_____

Dr. Seuss_____

Mary Pope Osborne_____

Pretend you are an author. How would you type your name into the online computer catalog?
Write your answer on the back of this paper.

Lesson 4—Library/Media Center, Team Teaching

Scavenger Hunt

Objective: Students will find answers to the questions using the online catalog. Students will find books on the shelves using titles and call numbers.

Language Arts National Standards

NL-ENG.K-12.4 COMMUNICATION SKILLS

Students adjust their use of spoken, written, and visual language (e.g., conventions, style, vocabulary) to communicate effectively with a variety of audiences and for different purposes.

NL-ENG.K-12.6 APPLYING KNOWLEDGE

Students apply knowledge of language structure, language conventions (e.g., spelling and punctuation), media techniques, figurative language, and genre to create, critique, and discuss print and nonprint texts.

NL-ENG.K-12.12 APPLYING LANGUAGE SKILLS

Students use spoken, written, and visual language to accomplish their own purposes (e.g., for learning, enjoyment, persuasion, and the exchange of information).

Skills

- Typing
- Searching the online catalog

Materials

- Worksheet copied for each student
- Pencils
- Title and call number cards (Option B)

Option A: Library/media center with twelve or more computers

Step 1. Students will gather at computers, with two or three students at each computer.

Step 2. Explain activity. Students will find answers to questions on the worksheet using the on-line catalog. Remind students that they have three choices for searching: author, title, and subject.

Step 3. Students complete worksheet.

Step 4. Share information with group.

Option B: Library/media center with fewer than twelve computers

Step 1. Divide class into two groups.

Step 2. One group will complete worksheet in Option A.

Step 3. The group not on computers will find books on the shelves using titles and call numbers. Students will review the location of books and call numbers in the library/media center. Tell students they will be looking for books on the shelves using the titles and call numbers.

Step 4. Media specialist will help students on the computers, and the classroom teacher will help students look for books on the shelves.

Teacher's Notes:

Scavenger Hunt

1. Find a book about dogs._____
    _____

2. Find a book written by Dr. Seuss._____
    _____

3. How many "cat" books do we have?_____
    _____

4. How many "dinosaur" books do we have?_____
    _____

5. Find a "weather" book._____
    _____

6. How many "horse" books do we have?_____
    _____

7. Find a book with "school" in the title._____
    _____

8. Do we have any books with "teacher" in the title?

    No _____Yes _____

    If yes, how many?_____

9. Find a book with "candy" in the title._____
    _____

10. Find a "spring" book you would like to read._____
    _____

Title and Call Number Cards

Clifford, the Big Red Dog E BRI	No, David! E SHA	George Washington B WAS	George W. Bush B BUS
Wayside School Is Falling Down F SAC	Socks F CLE	A Picture Book of Abraham Lincoln B LIN	Freckle Juice F BLU
Meet Samantha F ADL	Here We All Are B DEP	The Candy Corn Contest F GIF	Olivia E FAL
Green Eggs & Ham E SEU	Monster Trucks 629.223 KOO	Spiders 595.4 MUR	Eating Fractions 513.2 MCM
How to Be a Friend 158.2 BRO	Five Ugly Monsters E ARN	Jeff Gordon B GOR	Flags 929.9 ROW

Lesson 5—Classroom and Library/Media Center, Team Teaching

Searching and Locating Books

Objective: Students will type subjects, titles, and authors in computer, record titles and call numbers, and locate books on the shelf.

Language Arts National Standards

NL-ENG.K-12.4 COMMUNICATION SKILLS

Students adjust their use of spoken, written, and visual language (e.g., conventions, style, vocabulary) to communicate effectively with a variety of audiences and for different purposes.

NL-ENG.K-12.6 APPLYING KNOWLEDGE

Students apply knowledge of language structure, language conventions (e.g., spelling and punctuation), media techniques, figurative language, and genre to create, critique, and discuss print and nonprint texts.

NL-ENG.K-12.12 APPLYING LANGUAGE SKILLS

Students use spoken, written, and visual language to accomplish their own purposes (e.g., for learning, enjoyment, persuasion, and the exchange of information).

Skills

- Typing
- Searching an online catalog
- Learning the arrangement of the library/media center

Materials

- Worksheet copied for each student
- Pencils
- Blank overhead transparency and marker
- Overhead projector

Step 1. Classroom teacher and students will make a list of subjects, titles, and authors to use with the worksheet in the library/media center. Write list on a clear overhead transparency. List should reflect classroom curriculum.

Step 2. Classroom teacher takes the class and overhead transparency to the library/media center.

Step 3. Students will sit at the computers, with two or three students at each computer, or adjusted according to the number of work stations available. Project overhead transparency so all students can see the list.

Step 4. Media specialist explains the activity. Students take turns looking up items from the list, finding a book for each item, and recording the title and call number on their worksheets. Remind students that they need to make sure the book is on the shelf before writing it down.

Step 5. Media specialist and classroom teacher will rotate around the room to help as needed.

Teacher's Notes:

Title:_____
Call Number:_____

Title:_____
Call Number:_____

Title:_____
Call Number:_____

Title:_____
Call Number:_____

Title:_____
Call Number:_____

Title:_____
Call Number:_____

Lesson 6—Library/Media Center, Team Teaching

Relay Game

Objective: Students will type authors, subjects, and titles into the online catalog. Students will write down titles and call numbers and find books on the shelves.

Language Arts National Standards

NL-ENG.K-12.4 COMMUNICATION SKILLS

Students adjust their use of spoken, written, and visual language (e.g., conventions, style, vocabulary) to communicate effectively with a variety of audiences and for different purposes.

NL-ENG.K-12.6 APPLYING KNOWLEDGE

Students apply knowledge of language structure, language conventions (e.g., spelling and punctuation), media techniques, figurative language, and genre to create, critique, and discuss print and nonprint texts.

NL-ENG.K-12.12 APPLYING LANGUAGE SKILLS

Students use spoken, written, and visual language to accomplish their own purposes (e.g., for learning enjoyment, persuasion, and the exchange of information).

Skills

- Typing
- Searching on the online catalog
- Locating books on the shelves in the library/media center

Materials

- Dry erase board and marker
- Copy relay items, cut apart, and laminate
- Treat for winning team

Step 1. Divide class into two teams. Give the teams a few minutes to decide on a team name. Write teams' names on dry erase board.

Step 2. Evenly assign computers to each team.

Step 3. Explain relay game. Students will take turns typing on computers, recording titles and call numbers, and locating books on the shelves.

Step 4. Teams receive one point for every found book.

Step 5. Reward winning team.

Relay Items

Find a book written by Laura Ingalls Wilder
Find a book written by R. L. Stine
Find a book written by Michael Bond
Find a book written by Barbara Park
Find a book about Christmas
Find a book about cats
Find a book about dogs
Find a book about horses
Find a book about Halloween
Find a book about football
Find a book about cars
Find a book about trucks
Find a book about fish

Find a book written by Dr. Seuss

Find a book about Harriett Tubman

Find a book about George Washington

Find a book about Abraham Lincoln

Find a book about Martin Luther King, Jr.

Find a book about Laura Ingalls Wilder

Find a book about John F. Kennedy

Find a book about Benjamin Franklin

Find a book written by Cynthia Rylant

Find a book written by Audrey Wood

Find a book written by Norman Bridwell

Find a book written by Marc Brown

Find a book written by Eric Carle

Find a book written by Debbie Dadey

Resources

Videos

Using the Dewey Decimal System. Wynnewood, Penn.: Schlessinger Media, 2003.

Using the Library. Wynnewood, Penn.: Schlessinger Media, 2003.

Part Six

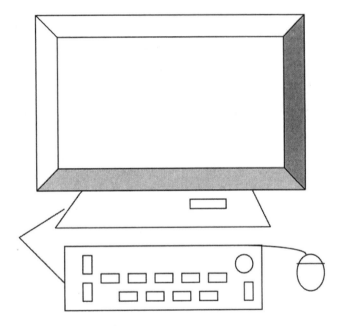

Internet Unit

Lesson 1—Library/Media Center, Team Teaching

Computer Equipment

Objective: Students will demonstrate their knowledge of computer equipment by labeling the important parts of the computer on the worksheet.

Language Arts National Standards

NL-ENG.K-12.4 COMMUNICATION SKILLS

Students adjust their use of spoken, written, and visual language (e.g., conventions, style, vocabulary) to communicate effectively with a variety of audiences and for different purposes.

NL-ENG.K-12.6 APPLYING KNOWLEDGE

Students apply knowledge of language structure, language conventions (e.g., spelling and punctuation), media techniques, figurative language, and genre to create, critique, and discuss print and nonprint texts.

NL-ENG.K-12.12 APPLYING LANGUAGE SKILLS

Students use spoken, written, and visual language to accomplish their own purposes (e.g., for learning, enjoyment, persuasion, and the exchange of information).

Skills

- Keyboarding
- Vocabulary computer terms

Materials

- Word cards for computer definitions (see word card page)
- Copies of worksheet and crayons
- Large, adult-size boot, stuffed mouse, plastic bug, picture of piano, CD case, house made of Lego blocks

Step 1. Cut out and laminate the word cards. Attach them to the items they match. All of the props should fit inside the boot.

111

Step 2. As students enter the library/media center, seat them around the computer station so a computer is visible and you have access to the screen and keyboard. Introduce the lesson using the boot full of props that you have prepared ahead of time. Explain that in the world of computers, some words take on different meanings. Remove each item from the boot, then read and discuss the definition and how it relates to the computer. Also point out the important features of the computer so that students get accustomed to the vocabulary and where the parts of the computer are located.

Step 3. Practice by calling on students to come and point out the mouse, keyboard, on and off button, screen, and so on.

Step 4. Pass out the worksheet and read the directions as a group.

Closure. The classroom teacher will rotate around to help as needed. During this time, the media specialist will help any students who may need more hands-on practice at the computer station.

Teacher's Notes:

Word and Definition Cards

Boot	**Starting up the computer**
Mouse	**Moves the cursor up and down and side to side**
CD	**Storage device to store programs and other data**

Word and Definition Cards

Bug	**When a computer gets sick**
House	**Web Address**
Keyboard	**Keys that tell the computer what to do**

Computer Equipment Worksheet

Color the computer by following the directions below.

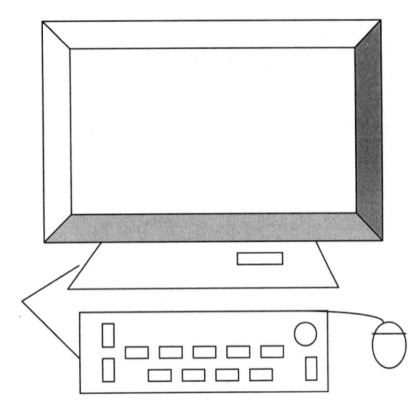

1. Color the computer screen blue.
2. Color the keyboard yellow.
3. Color the mouse red.
4. Color the on and off button black.
5. Color the CD drive orange.

Match up the definition with the correct word.

Boot   Keys that talk to the computer

Mouse   Starting up the computer

Keyboard   Moves the cursor

Lesson 2—Library/Media Center, Team Teaching

Web Page and Dictionaries

As students enter the library/media center, divide them into two groups. Part of the students will work with the media specialist on the computers, and the other half will work with the classroom teacher making student computer dictionaries.

Lesson 2A—Media Specialist

Objective: Students will demonstrate their knowledge of a Web page by pointing out the following: menu bar, back button, tool bar, address box, and scroll bar. By the end of the class, students will know how each of these functions on a Internet Web site.

Language Arts National Standards

NL-ENG.K-12.4 COMMUNICATION SKILLS

Students adjust their use of spoken, written, and visual language (e.g., conventions, style, vocabulary) to communicate effectively with a variety of audiences and for different purposes.

NL-ENG.K-12.6 APPLYING KNOWLEDGE

Students apply knowledge of language structure, language conventions (e.g., spelling and punctuation), media techniques, figurative language, and genre to create, critique, and discuss print and nonprint texts.

NL-ENG.K-12.12 APPLYING LANGUAGE SKILLS

Students use spoken, written, and visual language to accomplish their own purposes (e.g., for learning, enjoyment, persuasion, and the exchange of information).

Skills
- Keyboarding

Materials
- Word cards for computer definitions (see word card page)
- Copies of worksheet
- Have computers booted up and on a web site that is kid friendly (e.g., www.janbrett. com); another lesson will deal with typing in a Web address.

Step 1. Using the word cards, show students the back arrow, menu bar, address box, scroll bar, and tool bar. Stress the function of each item.

Step 2. Give out worksheets and explain how the students need to find the items on the computer and label the corresponding worksheet. Rotate among the students, helping as needed

Word and Definition Cards

Menu Bar	**Other things to do on the computer**
Tool Bar	**Short cuts to actions on the computer**
Scroll Bar	**Helps you view the whole page**

Back Arrow	**Returns you to the previous page**
Address Box	**Where you want to visit**
Cursor	**Marks the place of the mouse**

Find the items below on your computer. Label the picture on this worksheet.

Menu bar   Back arrow   Address box

Tool bar   Scroll bar

	File	Edit	View	Go				
			home					

www.janbrett.com

Internet Unit

Lesson 2B—Classroom Teacher

Objective: Students will make a computer dictionary.

Language Arts National Standards

NL-ENG.K-12.4 COMMUNICATION SKILLS

Students adjust their use of spoken, written, and visual language (e.g., conventions, style, vocabulary) to communicate effectively with a variety of audiences and for different purposes.

NL-ENG.K-12.6 APPLYING KNOWLEDGE

Students apply knowledge of language structure, language conventions (e.g., spelling and punctuation), media techniques, figurative language, and genre to create, critique, and discuss print and nonprint texts.

NL-ENG.K-12.12 APPLYING LANGUAGE SKILLS

Students use spoken, written, and visual language to accomplish their own purposes (e.g., for learning, enjoyment, persuasion, and the exchange of information).

Skills

• Computer Vocabulary

Materials

• Copies of dictionary cover for each student

• Blank paper for dictionary pages

Step 1. With the help of the students, make a list of new words that were introduced in Lesson 1). Use the word cards, to review those terms. Put the words in alphabetical order on the board and go through the following steps for completing the dictionary pages:

1. Write a new word at the top of each page (start with the vocabulary words from Lesson 1). Lesson 2 words can be added during classroom time.

2. Give a brief definition as it applies to computer language.

3. Use the word in a sentence.

4. Illustrate.

See the cover page for the dictionary booklet included in this lesson. As new words are introduced, pages can be added for the new terms (great classroom center time activity).

Student Dictionary Cover Sheet

My Computer Dictionary

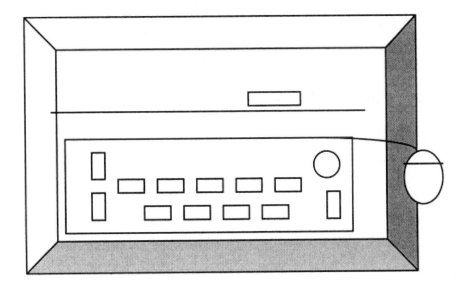

NAME_____

Lesson 3—Library/Media Center, Team Teaching

Changing Web Sites

Divide the class into two groups. The media specialist works with one group of students on the computers, and the classroom teacher works with the other group of students.

Lesson 3A—Media Specialist

Objective: Students explore a Web site and answer questions about it.

Language Arts National Standards

NL-ENG.K-12.4 COMMUNICATION SKILLS

Students adjust their use of spoken, written, and visual language (e.g., conventions, style, vocabulary) to communicate effectively with a variety of audiences and for different purposes.

NL-ENG.K-12.6 APPLYING KNOWLEDGE

Students apply knowledge of language structure, language conventions (e.g., spelling and punctuation), media techniques, figurative language, and genre to create, critique, and discuss print and nonprint texts.

NL-ENG.K-12.12 APPLYING LANGUAGE SKILLS

Students use spoken, written, and visual language to accomplish their own purposes (e.g., for learning, enjoyment, persuasion, and the exchange of information).

Skills

- Keyboarding
- Changing Web sites
- Exploring a Web site

Materials

- Computers
- Dry erase board and marker
- Worksheet copied for each student

Step 1. Review Lesson 2 by asking these questions:

Where is the address box, and what is it used for?

Which button is used to return to the beginning page?

What do you click on to move through a Web page?

Step 2. Introduce the "minimize," "restore," and "close screen" buttons. Use the word and definition cards.

Step 3. Tell students they are going to visit a Web site. Write the Web site address for author Kevin Henkes on the dry eraser board (www.kevinhenkes.com).

Step 4. Ask students to double click on the current address, which highlights the address. Students begin typing in the Web site address for Kevin Henkes. They will notice the initial address disappears as they start to type the new address.

Step 5. After the complete address has been typed, students will click on the "Go" button at the end of the address box.

Step 6. Kevin Henkes's Web site should now be displayed on the monitor. Look at the Web site and talk about the different areas and what you might find in each area.

Step 7. Explain the "Back" button using the word and definition card. Show students how to use the button by asking them to click on the mouse books on this Web site. Use the Back button to return to the opening page of the Web site. Allow students to explore Web site for a few minutes. After a few minutes, have students use the Back button to return to the opening page of Kevin Henkes's Web site.

Step 8. Tell students that they may want to visit Kevin Henkes's Web site another day. Use the definition and word card for bookmark. Explain how to use a bookmark. Students bookmark Kevin Henkes's Web site.

Step 9. Explain the worksheet. Students will use the Web site to answer the questions on the worksheet. Students will use the knowledge they have learned in the past three lessons to complete the worksheet.

Step 10. Students share answers.

Teacher's Notes:

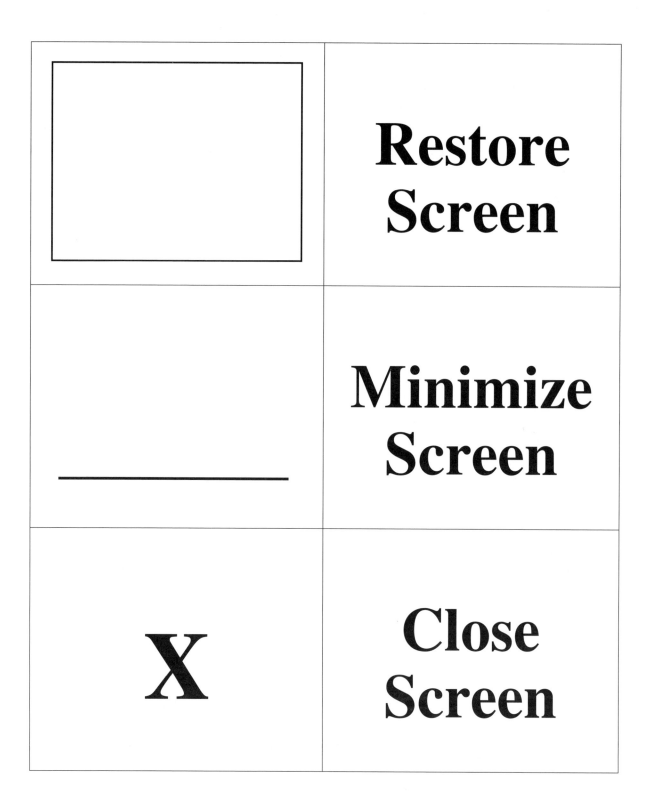

Word and Definition Cards

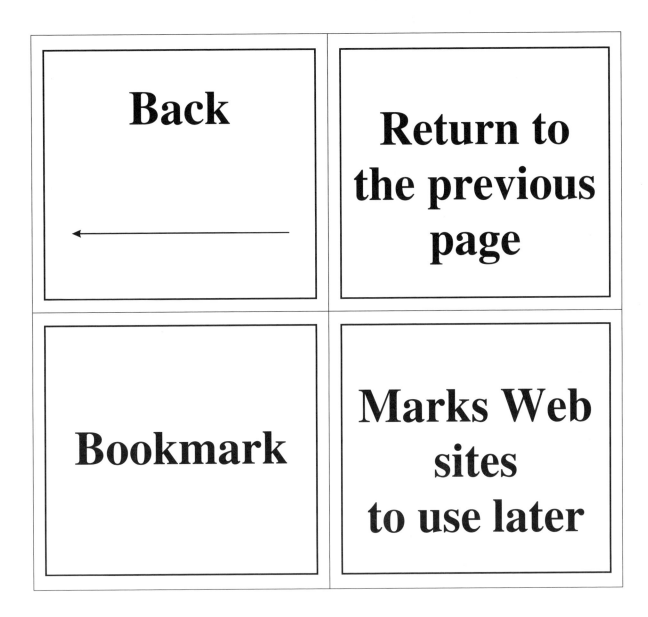

Back

Return to the previous page

Bookmark

Marks Web sites to use later

Kevin Henkes
www.kevinhenkes.com

Write the title of Kevin Henkes's first book.

_____

_____

Does Kevin Henkes have children? Yes_____   No_____
If yes, how many? _____

Write Owen's favorite thing.

_____

_____

Write the title of Kevin Henkes's newest book.

_____

_____

Write the title of one of Kevin Henkes's picture books.

_____

_____

Write the title of one of Kevin Henkes's mouse books.

_____

_____

Write the name of your favorite activity in Fun & Games.

_____

_____

Lesson 3B—Classroom Teacher

Objective: Students will listen to and discuss a book about the Internet.

Language Arts National Standards

ENG.K-12.4 COMMUNICATION SKILLS

Students adjust their use of spoken, written, and visual language (e.g., conventions, style, vocabulary) to communicate effectively with a variety of audiences and for different purposes.

ENG.K-12.6 APPLYING KNOWLEDGE

Students apply knowledge of language structure, language conventions (e.g., spelling and punctuation), media techniques, figurative language, and genre to create, critique, and discuss print and nonprint texts.

ENG.K-12.12 APPLYING LANGUAGE SKILLS

Students use spoken, written, and visual language to accomplish their own purposes (e.g., for learning, enjoyment, persuasion, and the exchange of information).

Skills

- Listening
- Comprehension

Materials

- A read-aloud book on computers or the Internet. Examples: *Arthur's Computer Disaster, In Touch Internet and E-mail,* or any other titles.

Step 1. Introduce the title of book and author. Explain to students that they will need to listen for words from Lessons 1 and 2.

Step 2. Read book.

Step 3. Talk about the book and write words on the board from Lesson 1. Review words and definitions that appear in the book.

Optional Activity. Students may complete the worksheet if time allows. Groups will trade places or return another day to complete tasks.

Teacher's Notes:

M	O	U	S	E	R	C	D	L	C	I	E
G	C	L	I	C	K	M	R	A	O	N	R
T	E	N	T	E	R	E	A	D	M	T	T
R	O	S	R	U	C	N	O	D	P	E	Y
L	L	O	R	C	S	U	B	R	U	R	O
W	E	B	L	S	A	B	Y	E	T	N	H
L	K	J	H	B	A	A	E	S	E	E	L
B	O	O	K	M	A	R	K	S	R	T	K
P	O	I	U	S	C	R	E	E	N	T	N

Word Bank

MOUSE	CLICK	KEYBOARD	SCREEN
CURSOR	TOOLBAR	ENTER	ADDRESS
BOOKMARK	MENUBAR	CD	WEB
INTERNET	COMPUTER	SCROLL	

Fill in the blanks for the following statements.

1. The back button is found on the _____.

2. Use a _____ to mark your Web site.

3. The mouse moves the _____ up and down and side to side.

4. When you want to visit a Web site, you need to type in an

    _____.

Lesson 4—Library/Media Center, Team Teaching

Search Engines

Divide students into two groups. One group will work on the computers with the media specialist, and the other group will watch a video with the classroom teacher.

Lesson 4A—Media Specialist

Objective: Students will become familiar with the term "search engine." Students will also practice typing subjects into a search engine.

Language Arts National Standards

NL-ENG.K-12.4 COMMUNICATION SKILLS

Students adjust their use of spoken, written, and visual language (e.g., conventions, style, vocabulary) to communicate effectively with a variety of audiences and for different purposes.

NL-ENG.K-12.6 APPLYING KNOWLEDGE

Students apply knowledge of language structure, language conventions (e.g. spelling and punctuation), media techniques, figurative language, and genre to create, critique, and discuss print and nonprint texts.

NL-ENG.K-12.12 APPLYING LANGUAGE SKILLS

Students use spoken, written, and visual language to accomplish their own purposes (e.g., for learning, enjoyment, persuasion, and the exchange of information).

Skills

- Keyboarding
- Searching on a search engine

Materials

- Word and definition cards

Gather students at the computers. The computers should be logged on to the Internet. Each school has a different system of logging onto the Internet.

Step 1. Review the address box and how to change a Web address.

Step 2. Explain the term "search engine" using the word and definition card. Tell students they are going to use a search engine and search for Web sites on a subject.

Step 3. Students double-click on the address box and begin typing www.yahooligans.com

Step 4. Click on the "Go" button at the end of the address box.

Step 5. Find the search box on the page. Type "snakes" in the search box and click on the word "search."

Step 6. Students will notice that the results of the search are numbered. Tell students they need to read the results and decide which Web site would give them the best facts.

Step 7. As a group, look at the results and decide which is the best Web site. Click on that site. Explore the Web site and discuss what you find.

Step 8. Go back and type in a new subject.

Lesson 4B—Classroom Teacher

Language Arts National Standards

NL-ENG.K-12.4 COMMUNICATION SKILLS

Students adjust their use of spoken, written, and visual language (e.g., conventions, style, vocabulary) to communicate effectively with a variety of audiences and for different purposes.

NL-ENG.K-12.6 APPLYING KNOWLEDGE

Students apply knowledge of language structure, language conventions (e.g. spelling and punctuation), media techniques, figurative language, and genre to create, critique, and discuss print and nonprint texts.

NL-ENG.K-12.12 APPLYING LANGUAGE SKILLS

Students use spoken, written, and visual language to accomplish their own purposes (e.g., for learning, enjoyment, persuasion, and the exchange of information).

Skills

- Reviewing Internet terms

Materials

- Video: *Using the Internet.* Wynnewood, Penn.: Schlessinger Media, 2003.

Prepare students for the video by telling them the title and that they are going to discuss the video afterward. Watch and discuss video.

Lesson 5—Library/Media Center, Team Teaching

Researching

Objective: Students will collect facts about a topic by using the Internet, encyclopedias, magazines, and other resource materials.

Language Arts National Standards

NL-ENG.K-12.3 EVALUATION STRATEGIES

Students apply a wide range of strategies to comprehend, interpret, evaluate, and appreciate texts. They draw on their prior experience, their interactions with other readers and writers, their knowledge of word meaning and of other texts, their word identification strategies, and their understanding of textual features (e.g., sound-letter correspondence, sentence structure, context graphics).

NL-ENG.K-12.8 DEVELOPING RESEARCH SKILLS

Students use a variety of technological and information resources (e.g., libraries, databases, computer networks, video) to gather and synthesize information and to create and communicate knowledge.

NL-ENG.K-12.12 APPLYING LANGUAGE SKILLS

Students use spoken, written, and visual language to accomplish their own purposes (e.g., for learning, enjoyment, and persuasion, and the exchange of information).

Science National Standards

NS.K-4.3 LIFE SCIENCE

As a result of activities in grades K–4, all students should develop understanding of

- The characteristics of organisms
- Life cycles of organisms
- Organisms and environments

Skills

- Researching
- Fact finding

Materials

- Each student will be assigned an ocean creature to research. (This topic can be tied into any applicable science curricular unit.)

Step 1. Media specialist. Briefly review the steps students need to follow to enter a Web site address and access the site. (See list of possible sites in the Resources at the end of this unit.)

Step 2. Classroom teacher. Brainstorm some other places to look in the library/media center for information. Write the list on the black board. This list could include Internet sites, encyclopedias, nonfiction books, and magazines.

Step 3. Classroom teacher. Hand out the worksheet and go over the things that the students are asked to collect by way of information. Model by writing a fact on the board. Stress that students need to use their own words after they have read the passage or information. The Internet site will give a picture of their sea creature that can be printed out. Count students off by fours and assign each group to a different section: computer, reference, nonfiction, and the magazine sections. After a short time, rotate the groups so that each has a turn at the computers.

Closure. Return to classroom and write reports.

Teacher's Notes:

Internet Unit
Lesson 5

Research Worksheet

Topic

What is address of the Web site you accessed?

_____

_____

List four awesome facts:

1. _____

_____

_____

2. _____

_____

_____

3. _____

_____

_____

4. _____

_____

_____

What other books did you use for this information?

_____

_____

_____

_____

Resources

Web Sites

www.seaworld.org
www.nwf.org/wildlife
www.nationalgeographic.com
www.yahooligans.com
www.janbrett.com
www.kevinhenkes.com

Video

Using the Internet. Wynnewood, Penn: Schlessinger Media, 2003.

Books

Brown, Marc. *Arthur's Computer Disaster.* Boston: Little, Brown, 1997.

Kazunas, Charnan, and Tom Kazunas. *The Internet for Kids.* New York: Children's Press, 1997.

Royston, Angela. *In Touch Internet and E-mail.* Chicago: Heinemann Library, 2002.

Simon, Seymour. *Bits and Bytes: A Computer Dictionary for Beginners.* New York: Harper and Row, 1985.

Wingate, Philippa. *The Internet for Beginners.* London, England: Saffron Hill, 1997.

Teacher's Guide

Internet Kids: A Guide to Skill-Building Lessons in the Elementary Grades. Cleveland, Ohio: World Almanac Education, 2000.

Part Seven

Thematic Unit

Thematic Unit

Introduction

Our thematic unit on insects and ants is an example of a unit that might be prepared through collaboration between the classroom teacher and the media specialist. It is a sample unit demonstrating how media specialists and classroom teachers can work together to tie curriculum to information literacy skills instruction. The unit is also a culminating unit that demonstrates everything students should be taught from this book.

We have designed this unit with grades 2 and 3 in mind, but the first three lessons can in fact be modified for first-grade use. This group of plans focuses on nonfiction and fiction books and how to recognize the differences. We also included basic research at the end of the unit. The format can be modified for future units.

Lesson 1—Library/Media Center. Introduction to unit on insects/ants: Nonfiction/fiction materials

Lesson 2—Classroom. Fiction Books: *Two Bad Ants*

Lesson 3—Classroom. Nonfiction Books: modeling fact finding

Lesson 4—Library/Media Center. Basic research on ants

Lesson 5—Library/Media Center. Extended research on another insect

Lesson 1—Library/Media Center, Team Teaching

Introduction to Unit on Insects/Ants

Objective: Students will be able to determine the difference between fiction and nonfiction ant books.

Language Arts National Standards

NL-ENG.K-12.3 EVALUATION STRATEGIES

Students apply a wide range of strategies to comprehend, interpret, evaluate, and appreciate texts. They draw on their prior experience, their interactions with other readers and writers, their knowledge of work meaning and of other texts, their word identification strategies, and their understanding of textual features (e.g., sound-letter correspondence, sentence structure, context, graphics).

Skills

- Word identification and definition

Materials

- Stack of ant books, both fiction and nonfiction (see resource list at the end of the unit). The media specialist will supply. If collection is limited, select other animals and insect books.

- Younger classes: select an animal nonfiction book and then a fiction book with a story character to whom the students will relate. You will need ones that demonstrate and contrast the differences between fiction and nonfiction material in a sharp distinct manner. (Example: *The Grouchy Ladybug* and a fact book on Ladybugs)

- Word cards for fiction and nonfiction with the definition on one side and the word on the other.

Front   Back

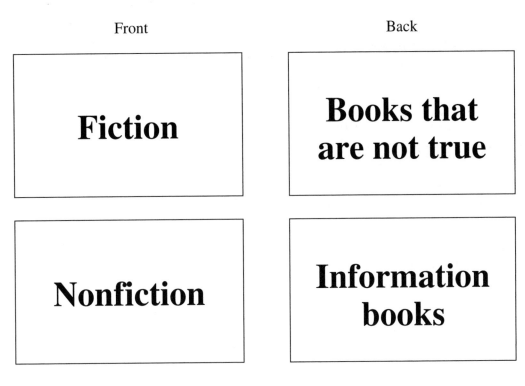

- T chart on paper with pen. (Nonfiction on one side and fiction on the other. Leave space underneath for students' comments.)

Nonfiction	**Fiction**

Step 1. The classroom teacher will introduce the word "fiction." Use the word card with the definition that you have prepared.

Step 2. The media specialist will choose a nonfiction book from the stack and page through the book. Be sure to share pictures and the way the book is laid out. Talk about the call number for nonfiction and the difference from fiction. Help the students make a list of important features of a nonfiction book. Examples: facts or information, pictures, sometimes real drawings or photos, glossary in the back, and the table of contents in the front.

Step 3. The classroom teacher discusses fiction in a similar fashion, drawing on students' comments to compose a list for the fiction side of the T chart. Examples: Not real, animals are talking, animals are dressed like people and are doing people-related things.

Step 4. The media specialist explains that the students will help put the stack of books into two piles, either nonfiction or fiction. Lay out the word cards so that the students can place the books into one pile or the other. Pick students to come to the front and choose a book. Let the class give a thumbs-up if the choice is correct. If a student has trouble, open the book and guide the class in helping make the correct choice. Encourage the students to look at the pages in the book. It is important that the students learn about the glossary and table of contents as well as other features of a nonfiction book. This can be a way to have them check if they are just guessing.

Lesson 2—Classroom

Fiction Books: Two Bad Ants

Objective: Students will be able to decide whether a story is fiction or nonfiction and also be able to place the events of the story in the proper sequence.

Language Arts National Standards

NL-ENG.K-12.3 EVALUATION STRATEGIES

Students apply a wide range of strategies to comprehend, interpret, evaluate, and appreciate texts. They draw on their prior experience, their interactions with other readers and writers, their knowledge of work meaning and of other texts, their word identification strategies, and their understanding of textual features (e.g., sound-letter correspondence, sentence structure, context, graphics).

NL-ENG.K-12.6 APPLYING KNOWLEDGE

Students apply knowledge of language structure, language conventions (e.g., spelling and punctuation), media techniques, figurative language, and genre to create, critique, and discuss print and nonprint texts.

NL-ENG.K-12.12 APPLYING LANGUAGE SKILLS

Students use spoken, written, and visual language to accomplish their own purposes (e.g., for learning, enjoyment, and persuasion, and the exchange of information).

Skills

- Sequencing
- Word meaning

Materials

- Book: *Two Bad Ants* by Chris Van Allsburg
- Colorful paper plates
- Cut-out story cards from the student worksheet or collect pictures that represent the different stages of the story (Make sure that you make up a title plate with the title and author on it for number one in the sequence. Color and prepare the pictures for the other plates.)
- T chart and word cards from Lesson 1.

Step 1. Read the story out loud to the class. Ask students to listen for all of the things that the two bad ants get into in their search for food.

140

Step 2. Review the story by asking the students for some of the problems that the ants had in their adventure.

Step 3. Line up the plates in mixed-up order. Choose students to place the cards in the proper sequence.

Step 4. Review the T chart from Lesson 1 and lead the students in a discussion of the things that made this a fiction or made-up story. How did they know that this was fiction?

Closure. Give directions for the worksheet pages. Students need to complete the sentences and color the pages. Cut and staple the pages in order as they happen in the text.

Teacher's Notes:

Two Bad Ants
by Chris Van Allsburg

Decorate your title page.

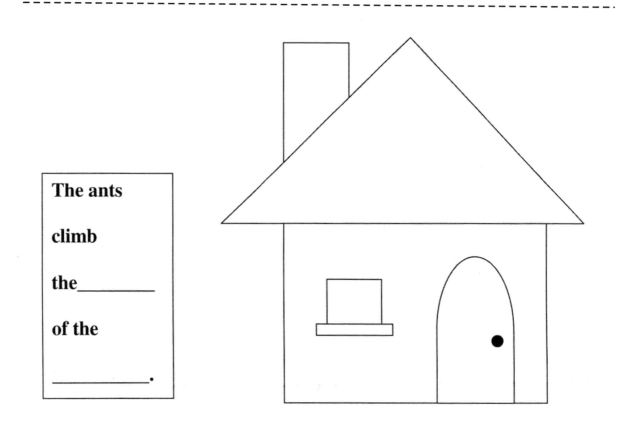

Inside the _____,
the temperature rises.

- -

The two little ants

eat too much of the

_____.

The ants cooled off in the
_____.

Draw what happens at the end of this story

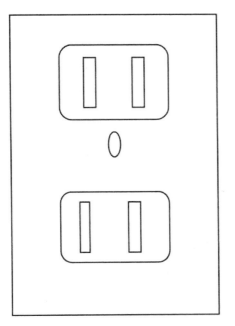

Draw the
ants and
what they do
in this part of
the story.

- -

Bitter

Hot

The coffee is _____, and it tastes
_____.

Lesson 3—Classroom

Nonfiction Books: Modeling Fact Finding

Objective: Students will be able to help make a class list of facts about ants after listening to a nonfiction book about ants.

National Science Standards

NS.K-4.3 LIFE SCIENCE

As a result of activities in grades K–4, all students should develop understanding of

- The characteristics of organisms
- Life cycles of organisms
- Organisms and environments

Skills

- Insect fact and identification

Materials

- Nonfiction book on ants (see Resources for suggestions)
- Nonfiction word card from Lesson 1
- Chart paper
- T chart from Lesson 1

Step 1. Build on the previous lesson by pointing out that in this lesson the ant book is a fact book, or nonfiction. Review with the students the T chart from Lesson 1 and point out the things that make a book nonfiction.

Step 2. Before reading the book, make a list of things that the students may already know about ants. Write these up on the chart paper.

Step 3. Read the book aloud to the students.

Step 4. Model for students what we are looking for in terms of facts. Introduce the idea that if we were writing a report on ants, we would not need complete sentences at this time but short bits of information that we learned from reading this book. Ask the students to help list the facts or information about ants that they remember from the book. Encourage them to list only things that are mentioned in the book.

Closure. Students return to seats and write their favorite fact out in a complete sentence.

Lesson 4—Library/Media Center, Team Teaching

Basic Research on Ants

Objective: Students will be able to write out facts about ants using books in the library/media center.

Science National Standards

NS.K-4.3 LIFE SCIENCE

As a result of activities in grades K–4, all students should develop understanding of

- The characteristics of organisms
- Life cycles of organisms
- Organisms and environments

Skills

- Note taking
- Researching

Materials

- Nonfiction books about ants from the library. Example: *World Book Student Discovery Encyclopedia,* Volume 1

Step 1. The classroom teacher will spend time reviewing the fact-finding strategies that were taught in the last lesson. Explain the worksheet and research process.

Step 2. Hand out materials and divide up the class into small groups of two or three, depending on the amount of resources you have available.

Step 3. The classroom teacher and media specialist rotate around the room and give help as needed.

Closure. Share facts

Teacher's Notes:

Label the antennae, head, thorax, and abdomen of the ant.

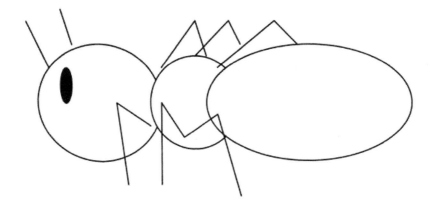

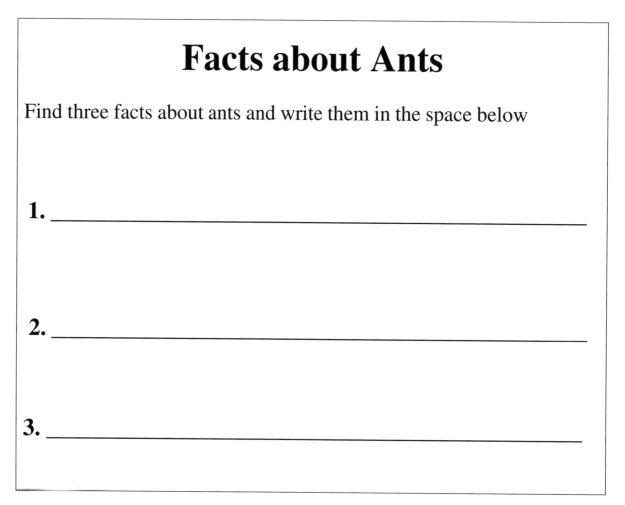

Facts about Ants

Find three facts about ants and write them in the space below

1. _____

2. _____

3. _____

Lesson 5—Library/Media Center, Team Teaching

Extended Research on Another Insect

Objective: Students will collect facts about an insect using books, magazines, and Internet sites.

Science National Standards

NS.K-4.3 LIFE SCIENCE

As a result of activities in grades K–4, all students should develop understanding of

- The characteristics of organisms
- Life cycles of organisms
- Organisms and environments

Lanuage Arts National Standards

NL-ENG.K-12.8 DEVELOPING RESEARCH SKILLS

Students use a variety of technological and information resources (e.g., libraries, databases, computer networks, video) to gather and synthesize information and to create and communicate knowledge.

Skills

- Note taking
- Researching

Materials

- Nonfiction books and encyclopedias
- Web sites:

    www.earthlife.net/insects/ants.html

    www.zoobooks.com

    www.kidsgowild.com

    www.wcs.org

Step 1. Students come to the library/media center with a copy of the worksheet and an insect assigned ahead of time by the classroom teacher. Possible insects to research: ladybugs, fleas, fireflies, spiders, beetles, bees, crickets, grasshoppers, mosquitoes, and cicadas.

Step 2. Students collect facts and fill out the worksheet on their insect.

Step 3. The media specialist and the classroom teacher will rotate around the room helping students select materials and information.

Closure. Students return to the classroom and share information. Worksheets are collected and compiled into a classroom book.

Note the extra "fun sheet" for the student who finishes ahead of the other students.

Teacher's Notes:

Research Worksheet

Name of insect_____

Where do these insects live?_____

How do they protect themselves from enemies?_____

_____

_____

_____

What do they eat? _____

_____

_____

Describe this insect _____

_____

Draw Your Insect

Ants

```
A  N  T  E  N  N  A  E
S  L  H  G  K  L  H  B
T  A  O  G  A  P  U  P
R  R  R  L  E  G  S  N
K  V  A  N  T  S  N  E
E  A  X  B  U  T  R  E
R  Y  N  O  L  O  C  U
A  B  D  O  M  E  N  Q
```

WORD BANK

LEGS	EGG	QUEEN
THORAX	PUPA	ANTS
COLONY	LARVA	ANTENNAE
	ABDOMEN	

Look up the words "colony," "pupa," "antennae," and "thorax" in the dictionary. Write the words and the definitions on the back of this paper.

ANTS

WORD BANK

six   two   colony   scent   strong   enemies

1. Frogs, toads, and anteaters are _____ of the ant.

2. Ants have _____ legs.

3. An ant has _____ antennae.

4. Ants live in a _____.

5. When ants leave the nest, they put down a _____

   trail so they can get back home.

6. Ants are small, but they are very _____.

Draw an ant colony.

Resources

Teacher Magazine Articles

Ants (Grades 2–3). *Teacher's Helper: Reproducibles for Your Classroom* 18, no. 3 (June/July 2001), pp. 3–12.

The Mighty Ant (Grades 1–3). *The Mailbox: The Idea Magazine for Teachers* 23, no. 3 (June/July 2001), pp. 4–9.

Nonfiction Titles

Cadder, S. J. *If You Were an Ant.* Englewood Cliffs, N.J.: Silver Press, 1989.

Dorros, Arthur. *Ant Cities.* New York: Harper & Row, 1987.

Pascoe, Elaine. *Ants.* Woodbridge, Conn.: Blackbirch Press, 1999.

Fiction Titles

Fleming, Denise. *In the Tall, Tall Grass.* New York: Henry Holt, 1991.

Pinczes, Elinor J. *One Hundred Hungry Ants.* Boston: Houghton Mifflin, 1993.

Van Allsburg, Chris. *Two Bad Ants.* Boston: Houghton Mifflin, 1988.

Web Sites

www.earthlife.net/insects/ants.html

www.zoobooks.om

www.kidsgowild.com

www.wcs.org

Bibliography

Books and Other Printed Materials

Adler, David. *A Picture Book of Amelia Earhart.* New York: Holiday House, 1998.

Adler, David. *A Picture Book of Eleanor Roosevelt.* New York: Holiday House, 1991.

Ants (Grades 2–3). *Teacher's Helper: Reproducibles for Your Classroom* 18, no. 3 (June/July 2001), pp. 3–12.

Brown, Marc. *Arthur's Computer Disaster.* Boston: Little, Brown, 1997.

Cadder, S. J. *If You Were an Ant.* Englewood Cliffs, N.J.: Silver Press, 1989.

Children's Atlas. New York: Facts on File, 2000.

Dorros, Arthur. *Ant Cities.* New York: Harper & Row, 1987.

Fleming, Denise. *In the Tall, Tall Grass.* New York: Henry Holt, 1991.

Geography for Life. Collingdale, Penn.: Diane Publishing, 1994.

Gormley, Beatrice. *First Ladies: Women Who Called the White House Home.* New York: Scholastic, 1997.

Internet Kids: A Guide to Skill-Building Lessons in the Elementary Grades. Cleveland, Ohio: World Almanac Education, 2000.

Kazunas, Charnan, and Tom Kazunas. *The Internet for Kids.* New York: Children's Press, 1997.

Lye, Keith. *The New Children's Illustrated Atlas of the World.* Philadelphia: Courage Books, 1999.

The Mighty Ant (Grades 1–3). *The Mailbox: The Idea Magazine for Teachers* 23, no. 3 (June/July 2001), pp. 4–9.

New Book of Knowledge. Danbury, Conn.: Grolier, 2002.

The New Millennium Atlas of the United States, Canada and the World. Milwaukee: Gareth Steven, 2000.

Pascoe, Elaine. *Ants.* Woodbridge, Conn.: Blackbirch Press,. 1999.

Pastan, Amy. *Eyewitness Books: First Ladies.* New York: Dorling Kindersley, 2001.

Pinczes, Elinor J. *One Hundred Hungry Ants.* Boston: Houghton Mifflin, 1993.

Rourke's World of Science Encyclopedia. Vero Beach, Fla.: Rourke, 1999.

Royston, Angela. *In Touch Internet and E-mail.* Chicago: Heinemann Library, 2002.

Rubel, David. *Scholastic Atlas of the United States.* New York: Scholastic, 2000.

Simon, Seymour. *Bits and Bytes: A Computer Dictionary for Beginners.* New York: Harper and Row, 1985.

Steele, Philip. *Scholastic Atlas of the World.* New York: Scholastic, 2001.

Van Allsburg, Chris. *Two Bad Ants.* Boston: Houghton Mifflin, 1988.

Wingate, Philippa. *The Internet for Beginners.* London, England: Usborne, 1997.

The World Almanac for Kids. Mahwah, N.J.: World Almanac Books, 2003.

The World Book Student Discovery Encyclopedia. Chicago: World Book, 2000.

The World Book Student Discovery Encyclopedia. Chicago: World Book, 2003.

Videos

Using the Dewey Decimal System. Wynnewood, Penn.: Schlessinger Media, 2003.

Using the Internet. Wynnewood, Penn.: Schlessinger Media, 2003.

Using the Library. Wynnewood, Penn.: Schlessinger Media, 2003.

Index

About the Authors

BRENDA S. COPELAND has been an elementary librarian for the past seven years in Palmyra School District, Palmyra, Pennsylvania. She earned her masters of library science degree from Kutztown University and her bachelors in elementary education at the University of Delaware.

PATRICIA A. MESSNER has been an elementary media specialist for the past sixteen years in the Lebanon City School District, Lebanon, Ohio. She earned her masters of education degree from Miami University, Oxford, Ohio, and her bachelors in elementary education at Asbury College, Wilmore, Kentucky.